D1261882

# FREEDOM FROM TRANSGRESSIVE KARMA

LECTURES ON THE INSTRUCTION ON REPENTANCE

# FREEDOM FROM TRANSGRESSIVE KARMA

Prime Dharma Master Kyongsan

Seoul Selection

# FREEDOM FROM TRANSGRESSIVE KARMA
Lectures on the Instruction on Repentance

Copyright © 2011 by Venerable Kyongsan
All Rights Reserved
No part of this book may be reproduced in any form without written
permission from the publisher.

Published by Seoul Selection
105-2 Sagan-dong, Jongno-gu, Seoul, Korea
Phone: 82-2-734-9567, Fax: 82-2-734-9562
Email: publisher@seoulselection.com
www.seoulselection.com

ISBN: 978-89-91913-81-3   03220
Printed in the Republic of Korea

The original Korean edition of this book was first published in 2005
by Dongnampoong.

# ❁ Contents

Preface     7

The Instruction on Repentance     14

Chapter 1 Why Do We Practice Repentance?     23

Chapter 2 The Meaning of Repentance     61

Chapter 3 Incorrect Repentance     103

Chapter 4 The Method of Repentance     131

Chapter 5 The Result of Repentance and Cultivation of the Way     179

Afterword     212

## NOTE

This book used the Revised Romanization system for Korean words appearing in the text. In the case of certain terms and names related to *Won*-Buddhism, however, it followed the McCune-Reischauer system adopted in the English-language versions of the *Won*-Buddhism scriptures.

# Preface

Each of us has lived through innumerable past lives. As the river waters flow implacably along their course, they gradually accumulate some type of sediment on their bed. In the same way, our pasts have flowed by, but there is something that lingers behind, constantly accreting.

Over the course of countless previous lives, the power of karmic action has accreted on the riverbed of our minds. At the same time, we have also accumulated things within the minds of others and accrued karmic power within the truth world. Some of us have acquired good habits and accumulated karma accordingly, and some of us have acquired bad habits and built up karma on that basis. Some of us have planted the fruits of happiness within others, and some of us have planted the fruits of transgressions and evil.

Those things acquired as past habits form the basis for our skills and our character, so that each of us possesses our own skills and our own character. We see people who are talented and people who lack talent, people who are skilled at writing and speaking and people who lack skill at these things. We also find those who are impatient and those who are slow, those who are introverted and those who are assertive. We often say that such talents and characters are innate. In reality, they are all formed out of habits instilled through repetition.

When we have performed many good works in our past lives and created happiness for others, we encounter positive affinity environments naturally in this life, as if by chance, and we receive the help of many people. Conversely, when we have done a great deal of harm to others in our previous lives, we endure difficult environments and trying conditions in this life.

How is your life? You may be suffering from want of talent or have many problems with your character. Some of us suffer due to poor affinities and relationships (with our family members, for example), and others of us are tormented internally by poor conditions. It is all so painful and trying that at times we are tempted to give up, but even that is not so simple. We may be suffering now on account of our character, or treated poorly due to our incompetence, or tormented by ill fortune, but is there hope for the future?

I remember a song that I often sang when I was a young boy: "The mill and the wheel turn merrily with a whirr, whirr, and a whirr, whirr / but a person's life turns in woe."

In life, the passing of one torment is frequently followed by the arrival of a new one, as though it were lying in wait. An agonizing existence, a life of suffering, a hopeless future—all of this stems from the karmic power that we built up through our own actions in the past. Just as a rock that falls from a high place rolls along according to its direction and force, our lives unfold through present and future according to the power of karmic action accumulated in past lives.

We must boldly effect changes in these painful and hopeless lives. The way for us to do so is through immediately repenting and cultivating the Way. Repentance is the only way to wash away the grime of past habit that has sullied our minds, to minimize the price that we pay for the transgressive karma of our many pasts, and to open up a happy future for ourselves.

Some people are living well today. They are welcomed by others for their consummate character, they have many things to do because of their talents, and they enjoy favorable conditions. Even these people, however, may find themselves suddenly and unwittingly falling apart or encountering a situation where no advancement is possible no matter how hard they work. At times, their very lives are shaken by some force outside of themselves.

Is our fate determined by God? By our ancestors? We know not who is responsible for our fate. Because of this, we cannot trust in the happiness of this moment, living in ignorance of the master of our destiny. It is as though we are driving a car with neither a license nor insurance.

In order to understand who the goddess of our fate is, we must repent and cultivate the Way. Once we have done so properly and definitely, we will understand the creator of destiny who determines our fate, and if we are simply able to control that creator, we can ensure eternal happiness for ourselves.

Lately, South Korea has been going through a restructuring period aimed at removing an economic bubble. As there are people here whose wealth exists only on paper rather than in reality, the process has been painful for many. Among those who cultivate the Way, we see some "pseudo-practitioners" whose airs outstrip the abilities of their minds; they direct their efforts merely at inflating their pretensions and drawing the attention of others, but they lack any actual mind-practice skills. Those who have been unable to rid themselves of this "bubble" are certain to face desolation in their later years and a trifling, empty next life.

We must reflect objectively over whether we are merely enjoying favorable treatment without real practice, or whether our treatment exceeds our current capabilities. If a bubble does exist, we must repent and cultivate the Way in order to remove it. With honest practice, we can eliminate the bubble.

For any practitioner, practice will only be sincere when his first step is repentance and cultivation of the Way. We students who follow the Buddhist way and are engaging in mind-practice must earnestly study the Instruction on Repentance bestowed upon us by the Founding Master so that we may rid ourselves eternally of transgressions and evil, and enjoy a happy eternal life—the eternal life of the buddhas and bodhisattvas.

When we carry out a ceremony, we recite the Instruction on Repentance. On occasion, we recite it to ourselves in the morning and evening. However, merely to recite it with our lips while our minds are elsewhere is blasphemy against the will of the great teacher who presented us this instruction. It is a foolish student who merely recites it without knowing its meaning, and it is an impious student who merely says the words without striving to put them into practice.

I begin these lectures with the hope that this will serve as an opportunity for us to show great piety to the Founding Master and all of the buddhas and sages of the past, present, and future by believing in the content of the instruction, awakening to it, and putting it into practice.

For ease of understanding, the text of the Instruction on Repentance has been divided into six sections.

- First, the motivation for repentance, i.e., why do we repent?
- Second, the meaning of repentance
- Third, the causes behind incorrect (incomplete) repentance
- Fourth, the method of repentance

- Fifth, the result of repentance.
- Sixth, some words of light reproach, particularly for the way that, in the view of high priests, the people of the world have taken too dim a view of repentance

Among these, the third, the section on incorrect repentance, and the sixth, the words of reproach on repentance, are similar in character and will therefore be discussed together. Also, I will endeavor to deliver an interpretation that is faithful to the words of the great teacher and that will be simple to put into practice.

I sincerely hope that through this lecture, the merciful dharma instruction of the Founding Master who gave us the Instruction on Repentance will guide you, me, and all living creatures as we rid ourselves forever of the suffering of transgressive karma and become true buddhas and bodhisattvas.

# The Instruction on Repentance

It is true that, in accordance with the Way of the alternating predominance of *yin* and *yang*, there is not a hair's breadth of uncertainty that those who perform good actions will subsequently receive a corresponding lifegiving reward, while those who perform evil actions will be repaid with a corresponding harmful retribution. But people who are repentant and reform their faults forever can free themselves from the power of these corresponding lifegiving and harmful karmic actions and command at will merits and transgressions. Therefore, all the buddhas and enlightened masters have unanimously opened this gateway of repentance.

As a rule, "repentance" is the first step in abandoning

one's old life and opening oneself to cultivating a new life, and the initial gateway for setting aside unwholesome paths and entering into wholesome paths. For people who repent from past mistakes and continue practicing wholesome paths day by day, past karma will gradually disappear and no karma will be made anew; good paths will come closer day by day and evil paths will recede of their own accord. Therefore, it says in a sūtra, "The mind's previous performance of evil is like a cloud covering the sun; the mind's subsequent generation of good is like the light of a bright lamp dispelling the darkness." Transgressions originally arise from the mind; they perforce will vanish once the mind is extinguished.

Karma is originally ignorance; it perforce will vanish in accord with the light of the wisdom of one's self-nature. Those of you who are moaning from the suffering of your transgressions: how can you not enter this gateway?

However, the foundations of transgressive karma are greed, hatred, and delusion. No matter how repentant you may be, if you subsequently repeat an evil action, there will never be a day when transgressions are extinguished. Furthermore, even though people who have committed serious transgressions and fall into the evil destinies may accumulate a certain amount of merit through temporary repentance, their transgressions will remain as such even while they receive merit according to their meritorious actions, so long as they leave the original greed, hatred, and delusion intact. This is like

someone who tries to cool down the water boiling in a large cauldron by pouring a little bit of cold water on top while letting the fire underneath continue to burn: the strength of the fire is strong while that of the cold water is weak, so the water will never cool down.

There are many people in the world who repent of their previous mistakes, but few who do not repeat those mistakes subsequently. Some people perform one or two types of merit through a temporary sense of repentance, but leave the greed, hatred, and delusion intact in their own minds; how can such persons hope to have their transgressive karma purified?

The method of repentance is of two types: repentance by action and repentance by principle. "Repentance by action" means that you sincerely repent from past

mistakes before the Three Jewels and practice day by day all types of wholesome actions. "Repentance by principle" means that, awakening to that realm in which the nature of transgressions is originally void, you internally remove all defilements and idle thoughts. People who seek to free themselves of transgressions and evil forever must practice both in tandem: externally, they must continue to practice all types of good karma while, internally, they must simultaneously remove their own greed, hatred, and delusion. In this wise, just as someone who tries to cool down the water boiling in a cauldron would pour a lot of cold water on top while putting out the fire burning underneath, so too, regardless of how much transgressive karma has been accumulated over hundreds and thousands of

eons, it will soon be purified.

Furthermore, if practitioners sincerely repent and cultivate the Way and achieve freedom of mind by awakening to the buddha in their self-nature, which is ever-calm and ever-alert, then they may choose any natural karma they please and command birth and death at will, so that there will be nothing to cling to or discard, and nothing to hate or love. The three realms of existence and the six destinies will all have the same one taste, and action and rest, adverse and favorable sensory conditions, will all be nothing other than samādhi. For such persons, myriad of transgressions and sufferings will vanish like ice melting in warm water, so that suffering is not suffering and transgressions are not transgressions. The light of the wisdom of their self-natures will shine

constantly, all the earth will become the ground of enlightenment and the pure land, where not even the slightest mark of transgression can be found either internally, externally, or in between. This is what we call the repentance of the buddhas and enlightened masters, and the Mahāyāna repentance. Only at this stage can we say that all transgressive karma has been brought to an end.

Recently there have been groups of self-styled enlightened ones occasionally appearing who, making light of the precepts and discipline and of cause and effect, have acted as they pleased and stopped as they pleased under the guise of "unconstrained action," thus sullying in some cases the gateway of the buddha. This occurs because they realize only that the self-nature is free from discrimination, but do not realize that it

also involves discriminations; how can this be knowing the true Way that transcends being and nonbeing? Furthermore, there are many people who think they have completed their practice just by seeing the nature and have no use for repentance or practice after seeing the nature. Even if seeing the nature has occurred, the myriad of defilements and all attachments are not simultaneously annihilated and, even if one has gained the three great powers and achieved buddhahood, one cannot avoid one's own fixed karma. One must pay close attention to this point and avoid falling into perverted views or making light of transgressive karma by misinterpreting the words of the buddhas and enlightened masters.

# CHAPTER 1

# Why Do We Practice Repentance?

It is true that, in accordance with the Way of the alternating predominance of *yin* and *yang*, there is not a hair's breadth of uncertainty that those who perform good actions will subsequently receive a corresponding lifegiving reward, while those who perform evil actions will be repaid with a corresponding harmful retribution. But people who are repentant and reform their faults forever can free themselves from the power of these corresponding lifegiving and harmful karmic actions and command at will merits and transgressions. Therefore, all the buddhas and enlightened masters have unanimously opened this gateway of repentance.

## Focus on

- The principle of alternating predominance of *yin* and *yang* that governs the universe
- Practice toward awakening to the fact that, because of this principle, the power of corresponding lifegiving and harmful karmic actions unfolds as our reality
- The reason we must rid ourselves of the power of corresponding lifegiving and harmful karmic actions

# The Way of the Alternating Predominance of *Yin* and *Yang*

The universe and nature operate in an orderly manner because of the existence of certain laws. The world proceeds through changes of creation and destruction, prosperity and decay, because there exists in it a principle without limit.

Men generally like women, and women generally like men. Not only among people but among animals as well, males and females are attracted to one another. This is something that is difficult to control through human willpower, for it is governed by a certain powerful force.

Heaven and earth have seasons of spring, summer, autumn, and winter. Slight differences may exist in places like the Equator or the Arctic Circle, but the changes of the four seasons are inescapable. Why should there be such changes according to the seasons? Besides this, day and night alternate within the universe. What is the basis that makes it so?

The universe and nature are characterized by a repeated cycle of change—being born, aging, sickening, and dying, and then passing again through birth, age, sickness, and death. If we look closely at our society and our state, we will see that they, too, exhibit such changes: prospering and prospering still more, only to decay and ultimately collapse. The mind of the human being also undergoes changes. Based on the sensory conditions that we encounter, thoughts arise, persist for some time, change, and finally vanish without a trace.

In this way, some peculiar, unseen principle exists such that men and women like one another; nature changes through the seasons of spring, summer, autumn, and winter; all things transform through birth, old age, sickness, and death; societies transform through creation and destruction, prosperity and decay; and our minds transform through a process of arising, abiding, transforming, and ceasing.

There is a peculiar, unseen principle that governs the universe and nature, society, and our lives. There is no question that this peculiar principle exists, but because it has no shape, it cannot be seen; because it is subtle, it cannot be grasped; and it manifests such inexhaustible creative transformations that it leaves not a trace behind.

Some time ago, I went hiking in the autumn. The mountain was tinted red from the top down along the slope. Some of the leaves were a deep coffee color, others tinged with green. In between was a mixture of tree trunks and rocks, the sounds of water and of wind—it felt as though I was enjoying a beautiful painting set to music. I wondered who it was that produced these beautiful works. I wanted to meet the artist, but I could not. I merely enjoyed the painting and the music and went on my way.

"Great enlightenment" comes when we have fully awakened to this peculiar principle. Thus it is said that Śākyamuni Buddha attained right enlightenment underneath the bodhi tree, the Founding Master attained great enlightenment at Norumok Hill, and Jesus Christ received the revelation at the River Jordan. All of them awakened to the peculiar principle hidden within this universe.

## Alternating Predominance of *Yin* and *Yang* and Retribution and Response of Cause and Effect

The Founding Master called this peculiar principle the "alternating predominance of *yin* and *yang*." He said that this was the principle that causes changes in all things, the principle that transforms the universe, the principle ensuring that those who commit transgressions are punished and those who create blessings receive blessings in turn, and the principle by which the world prospers and collapses.

From the cosmic perspective, we mainly use the term "principle of alternating predominance of *yin* and *yang*," and from a human perspective we use the term "principle of retribution and response of cause and effect." However, both of these represent one and the same principle.

In Chinese thought, the rules governing the universe are articulated as the principle of *yin* and *yang*, while in Indian thought the same rules are applied to human life and articulated as the principle of cause and effect. However, the principle of *yin* and *yang* and the principle of cause and effect are the same truth from the perspective of their governing the universe and human life.

In spring and summer, things emerge and expand. In autumn and winter, those same things hide away and contract. Because autumn and winter are characterized by contraction, their energy is said to be *yin* energy. Because spring and summer are characterized by expansion, their energy is said to be *yang* energy. Night, too, is a time of concealing and resting, and so *yin* energy flourishes, while day is a time of revealing and being active, and so *yang* energy flourishes. This can be explained in terms of our hands: when our fingers are fully clenched, this could be likened to the clustering of *yin* energy, and when they are fully splayed out, this could be compared to an abundance of *yang* energy.

All things within this universe are governed by *yin* energy at some times and by *yang* energy at others. In the spring and summer, they are controlled by *yang* energy and thus revive, grow, and show vibrant activity. Then, when the autumn and winter arrive, they are controlled by *yin* energy—all of their functions contract and shrink away, becoming invisible and concealed. This does not happen because all things wish it so. It happens because of the influences of *yang* and *yin* energy.

When we speak of these two energies fighting one another to victory, the one does not actually vanquish the other. *Yang* does what *yang* does; when the time comes, it cedes its place to *yin* energy, which flourishes until the time comes for it to yield to *yang* energy, and so on. Each conquers the other in a cycle of alternating predominance. A similar term for this is "mutual pushing": *yin* energy pushes *yang* energy, and vice versa.

The universe is immense in size and the myriad things within it diverse in kind, but they ultimately operate according to the power and providence of a single truth: the principle of alternating predominance of *yin* and *yang*. This peculiar principle of heaven and earth is the very master of heaven and earth. It is what actually governs heaven and earth, all things, and all human affairs. Nothing within heaven and earth can ever escape from this principle.

This principle is called "the principle of cause and effect" and "the Dharmakāya Buddha." It is called "the Il-Won-Sang Truth," "the Way," and "heaven." The truth that forms the foundation prior to this "principle of alternating predominance of *yin* and *yang*" is called "the principle that neither arises nor ceases." It is not the case that the principle that neither arises nor ceases exists separately from the principle of alternating predominance of *yin* and *yang* (or retribution and response of cause and effect). Rather, we use the term "principle that neither arises nor ceases" when speaking in terms of the principle's essential nature aspect, and we use the term "principle of alternating predominance of *yin* and *yang*" when speaking in terms of its functional aspect.

So when we speak of the "principle of alternating predominance of *yin* and *yang*," it is naturally grounded in the "principle that neither arises nor ceases" that is its essential nature. And when we speak of the "principle that neither arises nor ceases," this is accompanied by the "principle of alternating predominance of *yin* and *yang*" that is its function. We might say that they represent the two sides of a single coin.

In the Instruction on Repentance, however, the Founding Master speaks more of the "principle of alternating predominance of *yin* and *yang*" than of the "principle that neither arises nor ceases." This is because the instruction's main content has to do with the clear operations of the truth, such as being punished when one transgresses and being blessed when one creates blessings.

Those who create blessings may not wish to receive blessings in kind, but the marvelous principle of alternating predominance of *yin* and *yang* that is master of this universe performs a clear calculation and delivers the blessings anyway. Likewise, it brings sure punishment to those who commit transgressions.

In this way, the presence of the "principle of alternating predominance of *yin* and *yang*" ensures that all living creatures receive corresponding lifegiving and harmful karma according to the way in which they have behaved. The principle of *yin* has the characteristic of contraction and the preservation of seeds. If I enjoy a great deal of grace from someone, I develop gratitude toward him, and that mind of gratitude takes the form of a corresponding lifegiving karmic cause for that person—a karma seed of grace. Conversely, if he does me harm, thoughts of hatred toward him arise within my mind. Those thoughts gather together to form a corresponding harmful karmic cause—the seed of harm toward that person.

The things preserved as wholesome and unwholesome karmic causes in this way will inevitably manifest themselves as effects when their time comes. The karmic cause that forms the seed of resentment is realized through the effect of our doing harm to the object when we encounter him. If someone plants a seed of gratitude, this inevitably manifests itself as grace. The principle whereby actions are realized as these wholesome and unwholesome effects is possible because of the *yang* principle.

Thus *yin* is the cause and *yang* the effect. As such, the principle of alternating predominance of *yin* and *yang* in the universe is the same as the human principle of retribution and response of cause and effect. For this reason, we use the term "principle of retribution and response of cause and effect" when speaking of the principle whereby humans give and receive in kind.

## The Three Properties of the Principle of Alternating Predominance of *Yin* and *Yang*

Thus far, I have explained how the existence of the principle of alternating predominance of *yin* and *yang* serves to create and foster all things, to kill and preserve them as its truth operates, and how it gives blessings when humans create blessings and gives punishment when humans commit transgressions.

When we are practicing repentance after committing a transgression, it is easy for us to believe that it is enough simply to ensure that we do not commit other transgressions and to work to create blessings. However, it is not as simple as this. To begin with, not only is it difficult to know what constitutes a transgression and what constitutes a blessing, it is also possible to deceive our conscience when others are not looking. Ultimately, ours will only be true repentance practice when we understand the principle of alternating predominance of *yin* and *yang*—the principle of transgressions and blessings. We must therefore study the principle of the universe.

Once we have a deep understanding of the principle of alternating predominance of *yin* and *yang*, repentance practice becomes much easier. I will explain to you about a few of the properties of this principle.

First, the principle of alternating predominance of *yin* and *yang* that is master of heaven and earth and all things is truly vast. It is akin to a mother who clutches everything to her breast— heaven and earth, nature, the solar system and the galaxies— without abandoning any one of them.

Also, this principle is very radiant. The number of things that exist is too great to count, and there is a limitless diversity in what they do. Yet one bright-eyed person sees and understands every one of them without exception. The Founding Master called this the "consciousness of heaven and earth."

It sees even the small transgressions that we commit where no one sees us, and it sees all of the good that we do for others in the darkness and gives us corresponding blessings in kind.

Right now, it sees all of my sincere commitment in delivering this lecture, and it sees into the minds of every one of you who are listening to it. In a sense, it is as though we are being monitored at all times by the bright eye of a truth buddha. It is frightening, but also unavoidable.

Next, the principle of alternating predominance of *yin* and *yang* is a creator and an effector of creative transformations that is capable of doing anything.

Look at the grandeur and greatness of heaven and earth and of nature. See how it requites all things appropriately according to their individual characteristics. Witness the beauty of the flowers on a warm spring day, the majesty of the sun rising in the east, the sad beauty of the setting sun. Behold the frail and delicate flowers and the tiny insects going about their lives. All of these are creative transformations of the truth.

We live within the vast bosom of the truth in which *yin* and *yang* alternately predominate, and within the grace of radiant discrimination and creative transformation. We should therefore be fully aware of this truth, repent of the transgressions that we have committed, and go about creating good karma.

# REWARD AND RETRIBUTION FOR GOOD AND EVIL ACTIONS

If I should do something beneficial for someone or engage in some action that helps society, the one who enjoys the benefits is certain to bring a corresponding amount of blessings to me at a later time. He and I will form a relationship of mutual preservation. Conversely, if I do something harmful to him, he will bring me some misfortune at a later time, and we will form a relationship of giving and receiving animosity.

In this way, if we wonder what it is that acts to bring about the result in which happiness comes to those who perform good actions, and unhappiness to those who perform evil actions, we will see that it is the principle of alternating predominance of *yin* and *yang*, the Il-Won-Sang Truth, that does so.

When we perform a good action, we may not necessarily seek to receive in kind, but this principle calculates precisely and gives us exactly that amount in return. Likewise, when we commit a transgression against someone and then run off and hide in the hope that we will not pay the price for our transgression, it finds us without fail and delivers a corresponding punishment. The term "principle of alternating predominance of *yin* and *yang*" is a concrete expression of that truth. Some people believe in the existence of this principle but are not certain, some deny its existence, and some have vividly awakened to it.

Ordinarily, the majority of people fail to understand this truth and deny it. Most people who believe in religions are not certain, but they live their lives with faith according to the instruction of teachers. However, there are also people who have vividly awakened to this principle and put it into practice and are creatively embodying it within their lives and their society.

Through this lecture, let us believe, understand, and practice, so that we may escape from transgressions and evil and enjoy eternal blessings and happiness.

## Who Performs Good and Evil Actions?

I have already explained how the truth of alternating predominance of *yin* and *yang* is what brings blessings and happiness to the person who has performed good actions and punishment to the person who has performed bad actions. I believe that you have sufficiently understood this.

We should consider, however, who the agent is that performs these good and evil actions. If someone does not perform any good actions, the truth cannot give him any blessings, no matter how much it may wish to, nor can it give punishment to the person who does not perform evil actions, no matter how much it may want to do so.

The truth principle of alternating predominance of *yin* and *yang* gives corresponding harmful and lifegiving retribution to people in a somewhat passive way according to their actions. We must therefore consider who the agent is that creates transgressions and blessings.

If we wonder who it is that gives benefits to some and harm to others, we will see that it is ultimately our own mind and body that operate on that person to perform good and evil actions. In the end, I become the actor and operate, whether through good actions or evil. So if I instill the habit of performing good actions when I use mind and body, I will come to perform good actions continuously and receive happiness forever. Similarly, if I develop the habit of performing evil actions, I will engage in evil actions at all times and suffer harm.

At the factories where archery arrows are made, the makers study how to make arrows that are sharper and hit the target well, and they manufacture the arrows accordingly. But at the factory where shields are made, the makers consider how to block the sharper arrows and avoid suffering injury when they make their shields.

People, too, possess a diverse range of factories. Some create products that give continuous benefits to others through body, words, and mind, while others create products that give continuous harm to others through body, words, and mind. Still others alternately manufacture products that give benefits to others at some times and give harm to others at other times. In some cases, they benefit certain people but harm others.

All of us have the capability to create happiness or unhappiness, peace or discord. In response to the six kinds of sensory conditions that we experience from outside—what we see, hear, smell, taste, touch, and think—the six organs of our eyes, ears, nose, tongue, body, and mind function to generate products both wholesome and unwholesome.

For instance, some of us hear with our ears the sound of a song that makes us think, "How beautiful," and we send our praise and thanks to the singer. Conversely, some of us have thoughts of "This song isn't any good," and we criticize and disparage the singer. Of course, there is no way of knowing whether praise or disparagement is appropriate. But when our consciousness hears the sensory conditions of the song through the ears, produces a mind of "liking" or "not liking," and either praises or criticizes that person, this is not something that another person is making us do. It is our own mind that is doing it, through the six sense organs present within us.

In this way, we encounter sensory conditions and produce happiness or unhappiness depending on how we use our minds. Thus, the creator of our own happiness and unhappiness is the self and the functioning of the mind.

Śākyamuni Buddha said that all things are the creation of one mind. The creation of happiness and unhappiness depends on the functioning of each person's mind, and all of us may respond with positive or negative thoughts to the same environment according to our own determinations. The functioning of the mind can make us into a buddha or into a wicked person, and blessings or agonizing torment may come our way depending on how we have used our minds. Thus, our own mind is the creator that determines our happiness and unhappiness.

Only when we understand for certain that our minds are our creators can we engage in true repentance practice. If a practitioner of repentance believes that his misfortune is caused by another person, or by bad luck or fortune, he will not try to reform his behavior. And if he believes that there is an absolute somewhere above that deals punishment to him, he will merely try to seek blessings from it rather than changing his own mistaken behavior. Thus the person engaged in repentance practice must have a clear awareness that his mind is his creator before he can engage in sincere repentance.

## The Self-Cause and Self-Effect of Good and Evil Actions

When we use our six sense organs to engage in some behavior directed at another person, two types of fruits are formed. Here is an example. Suppose that I wholeheartedly sing a beautiful song for a group of people. I have given pleasure to the minds of the listeners, and in so doing I have planted fruits of good within them. Also, because I have sung the song, a habit or talent for singing will also be planted within my mind.

As another example, suppose that I have cursed at someone. Accordingly, seeds of the bad habit of cursing will be sown within my mind, while seeds of harm directed against me will be sown within the mind of the person who heard my curses. We must understand this well.

The cause and effect that we sow for ourselves in this way might be called "self-cause and self-effect." We sow seeds of good or bad habits, and these ultimately manifest themselves through the result of a good or bad person. The seeds that we sow with ourselves build up to shape our own character, and for this reason they are called "self-cause and self-effect."

A few years ago, I was greeted by two *Won*-Buddhists, a husband and wife couple. The husband described his personality by saying, "I'm so hot-headed that it's like setting fire to a dry leaf."

Hearing this, his wife said, "Is that all? It's more like tossing a lit match on gasoline." And she went on to recount how much difficulty she endured in her younger days on account of her impetuous husband. I asked him how long he had had this impetuous character, and he said that it had been with him since birth. In other words, he had been impetuous from the very moment he entered this world.

If we produce impetuous thoughts once, and then again, over and over, a habit of impetuousness will form within our minds, and we will become instilled with an impetuous character that we can do nothing about. All of you listening to this lecture have your own character. Some have the character of the slowpoke, others are diligent, still others assertive, passive, and so forth. All of these are things that you have created for yourselves, formed for yourselves, brought upon yourselves.

Not only characters but gifts as well differ from person to person. A skillful person can easily fix something that is broken. In many cases, however, a person who lacks skill will try to fix something only to end up breaking it further. We also find people who possess a gift for music or a gift for writing. I believe that our *kyomu* (*Won*-Buddhist clergy) are likely to have a talent for speaking in their next lives as well. I speak a lot now myself, and I am a little worried that I will be someone talkative in my next life.

Aptitude tests for schoolchildren show a variety of different strengths, including those for science and engineering, the humanities, arts, and athletics. Two brothers may have completely different aptitudes. If someone spends a lifetime in banking, performing a vast number of calculations, this will build up and perhaps lead to an aptitude for finance. Someone who studies literature and spends a lifetime writing will likely have an aptitude for the humanities.

Each person also has a slightly different bearing as well. Some of us are innately graceful, while others are coarse. All of this is determined by the values that person possesses and the way in which he has trained the habits of his mind.

Thus the character, gifts, and bearing that we possess today are not created by anyone else. We have shaped them ourselves by instilling habits over the course of our previous lifetimes. We might term this "self-cause and self-effect," or "self-forming through self-training." This means that we have formed our own character by instilling habits in ourselves.

The character, gifts, personality, and values that we form over odd occasions become the foundation for our creating blessings and committing transgressions in our dealings with others. If, since far back in our past, we have steadily worked to shape an outstanding character, creating blessings for others will be easy for us. But if we have shaped a coarse character, we will often find ourselves committing transgressions against others.

Still, we cannot immediately conclude that someone with an outstanding character will always create blessings and someone with a coarse character will always commit transgressions. Even those of outstanding character can occasionally commit transgressions and evil against others, and even those of coarse character can do good things for their own family members or for other people.

When we have instilled an outstanding character or a coarse character through self-cause and self-effect, we are likely to create blessings or to commit transgressions based on what we have instilled. But it cannot be said that this is always the case. Even if we are possessed of an outstanding character, we are unlikely to create blessings when we do not direct our actions toward others. Even a wicked person will seldom commit transgressions if he does not act toward others.

When we train our character with self-cause and self-effect and with self-forming through self-training, we are like an athlete who develops outstanding skills through diligent practice. But just as the athlete with outstanding capabilities must obtain good results by showing those capabilities on the field, the person with an outstanding character must act in reality to bring benefits to others if he is to create genuine blessings.

The person with good tools will find it easy to produce great results in his work, while the one with primitive tools will not only find it difficult to generate effects commensurate to his effort, but at times he will actually suffer as a result of his tools.

The paramount principle of repentance is the process of understanding the principle of self-cause and self-effect, determining whether our character, gifts, values, and bearing make it easy for us to create blessings or commit transgressions, and improving them in order to make it easy for ourselves to create blessings.

## The Consequences of Other-Directed Cause and Effect

By "other-directed cause and effect," we are referring to rewards or retribution that returns to us as a result of what we have planted in the minds of others through our actions.

Before he begins farming, a farmer chooses his seeds. Some of the seeds chosen will be superior, while others will be of lesser quality. He sows these seeds in his field and cultivates them. He tends to them, pulling weeds and applying fertilizer, and when the time comes he harvests the fruit. At this time, the person who has sown lesser-quality seeds will frequently have lesser-quality fruit, and the person who has sown superior seeds is likely to have superior fruit. Moreover, he may have a greater or lesser yield depending on his efforts at weeding and fertilizer application.

In the same way, our actions are planted in the minds of others, and we reap the results. This could be called "other-directed cause and effect." If I help someone out financially, he will harbor a deep sense of gratitude within his mind. This, in turn, will manifest itself through the result of his bringing me happiness in the next life.

If, on the other hand, he has caused me great pain, forcing me to stifle my rage and endure suffering, the actual dealing of pain may have taken place at that particular time, but an emotion of animosity toward him is sown within my mind, and at some later time I will find myself in a situation where I am forced to take revenge. I will therefore pay him back for what he has done.

Each person has different affinities. I sometimes officiate at weddings, and people generally come to me before the ceremony and pay their respects. I offer them my congratulations and provide some instructive words. Occasionally, I go on to ask the couple how they met and how they arrived at marriage to one another. When I ask them this, they smile at one another and say that it "just happened."

Why should it be that out of all the people in the world, two particular people should form an affinity and come together as husband and wife? It is because the two of them have met innumerable times over the course of previous lives, forming a tender relationship in the process, and the result of that affinity is their meeting in this life to form the affinity of husband and wife.

Affinities can become correspondingly harmful when people give and take things that are not good, and they can become correspondingly lifegiving when people exchange only good things. The wholesome and unwholesome causes that both have planted over the course of their frequent meetings bear fruit, and this becomes the force behind their meeting again in this life.

Oddly enough, most people exchange grace with their family members without any particular attention to the calculation of benefits and losses. Among married couples, among parents and children, and among siblings, people share pain and happiness without any particular conditionality, and without any question of wishing to do so or not. This is the result of unconditional exchanges that took place through the formation of close relationships over previous lifetimes, which have led them to live together as family in this one.

In this world, we encounter people who share their pains and happiness unconditionally with friends and colleagues as they live their lives, and we see relationships where one side is endlessly sacrificing. This, too, can be understood as giving in this life what one received in a previous one.

Thus it is called "other-directed cause and effect," since it means reaping seeds of good or evil that we planted in another person. It is also called "receiving as we have created," since we are sowing and cultivating seeds of good or evil in others and ultimately reaping the fruits of this.

It is also something akin to our own alter ego, through which the seeds of good and evil that we have planted in the mind of another through our actions toward him grow within his mind-field and the results come back to us. A farmer once said, as he reaped crops that he had cultivated with the sincerest of care, "This rice is like my alter ego, my own child."

We make judgments before speaking and acting toward other people. These words and actions are stored up within the other person as our alter ego before returning to us when the time comes as a reward or as retribution. When someone retaliates against us, we must understand it to be something that we left with that person coming back to us once again, and we must submit to it stoically.

Over the course of innumerable previous lives, we have sown seeds of good and evil in many sentient beings. We have sown seeds of good and evil in people, in animals, and in microorganisms, at times consciously and at other times unconsciously. The person who has instilled bad habits and sown mainly bad seeds will receive corresponding retribution from many animals and microorganisms, while the person with the character of a buddha or a bodhisattva will have sown mainly wholesome seeds and will live in a paradise where blessings never run dry.

The meaning of our current study of the Instruction on Repentance is that if, due to ignorance of the truth of cause and effect, we sowed seeds that are not good in other sentient beings in our past lives, we should repent of this and reform our behavior so that we are no longer the type of person who commits transgressions and evil that cause pain in the hearts of others.

## Where Is the Karma That We Create Preserved?

Earlier, I explained how we are our own creators, shaping our character by creating self-cause and self-effect through our mental and bodily functioning, and how we receive from others corresponding lifegiving and harmful rewards and retribution, good and evil, through the creation of other-directed cause and effect.

However, we must understand where the self-karmic retribution (self-formed through self-training) that we create with objects and the other-directed karmic retribution (received as we have created) that we create in others are stored up before making its eventual appearance. The Instruction on Repentance tells us that we subsequently receive a corresponding lifegiving reward or corresponding harmful retribution. As the next part of the sequence, we must learn where the karmic retribution thus created is preserved, and when it will come back to us as a reward or retribution.

The results of the karma that we create with our body and mind do not appear right away. Rather, they are stored away somewhere for a time before manifesting themselves. Just as we put the seeds from the grain harvested in the autumn in a granary or jar and store them away before taking them out to cultivate with the next year's spring planting, the seeds of karmic power lie stored away in someone for a time before manifesting themselves when their time comes. We see the same principle when we eat: sometimes, the nutrients in our food do not immediately manifest themselves as energy but are stored in the liver for a time before emerging.

The karma seeds of good and evil that we create with our body, words, and minds are stored in the deepest part of our minds. This place is called the "storehouse consciousness," or, in Sanskrit, the "eighth *ālaya-vijñāna*."

Our minds broadly consist of three layers. The first of these is the surface consciousness, which arises according to sensory conditions. We call this the "sixth consciousness." Next, there is the "self consciousness," also called the "seventh (*manas*) consciousness," which refers to a mind deeper than the six sensate consciousnesses. Finally, there is the "eighth consciousness," which is like a karma pocket or karma storehouse that holds and stores all of our karmic retribution.

It will be helpful for our repentance practice if we understand the world of the mind, so I will explain about the eighth consciousness in a bit more detail. We humans have six sense organs. These are similar to the different ministries within a nation's government that conduct the affairs of the state. The six organs are our eyes, ears, nose, tongue, body, and mind. Of these, the first five correspond to the body. These are called the "five prior consciousnesses," as they are said to be organs prior to awareness.

Outwardly, these five consciousnesses take as their objects five types of sensory conditions. The eyes perceive colors and shapes as objects (the color world), the ears perceive the pitch and rhythm of sounds (the auditory world), the nose perceives smells (the olfactory world), the tongue perceives various flavors (the gustatory world), and the body perceives various sensations (the tactile world). The five types of perception here—through the eyes, ears, nose, tongue, and body—are called the five prior consciousnesses.

When the information perceived by these senses is transmitted to the sixth consciousness, that consciousness processes the imformation from the sensations entering from outside and, based on previously accumulated experiences, judges their good or evil, right or wrong, benefits or harm, before conveying an order to the five organs and generating action. The experiences and conceptions built up within the consciousness are referred to as "dharma-*viṣayā*," or dharma objects.

While the eyes, ears, nose, tongue, and body respectively take colors, sounds, scents, tastes, and sensations as their objects, the consciousness acts upon information coming in from outside and experiential knowledge (dharma objects) that is already present within. In other words, whereas the sense organs function simply and mechanically, the consciousness receives things from the outside and combines them with things inside to create various different thoughts. On top of this, we have the ability to think by ourselves even if we are alone, without any information coming in from outside. This is what is called the "sixth consciousness."

If we step inside this world of consciousness, however, we will find at the bottom something called the "seventh consciousness" or "*manas* consciousness." This is the soul, the true self within our body. This soul exists within the body and commands it through the consciousness.

At the center of the soul is self-love, which is constantly seeking to protect the self. This self-love manifests itself as surface consciousness, including greed, anger, and delusion. Thus the consciousness manifested on the surface takes its orders from the soul that exists at its foundation.

Next, there is the eighth *ālaya-vijñāna*, located in the deepest reaches of the consciousness. This is the world of truth. This world of truth, the *ālaya* world, is where we store the karma seeds, good and evil, created through the functioning of our soul and consciousness. Every seed we have created, good or evil, is stored away in the storehouse that is the *ālaya*. Once stored, it is beyond the scope of our soul or consciousness, subject instead to equitable administration by the truth.

This *ālaya* consciousness exists separately from the world of values as humans commonly conceive of them, where virtue is appreciated and evil is detested. It serves to store all karma seeds equally, good and evil alike. When the good and evil karma seeds are stored, a decision is made as to when they will encounter an affinity and germinate to manifest themselves as effects.

We speak of two main schedules by which this karma manifests itself as an effect. One is non-fixed karma, and the other is fixed karma.

With non-fixed karma, the seeds of karmic cause are weak because the karma was weak in its creation. In such cases, it has not been decided precisely when it will manifest itself.

Fixed karma is very powerful in its creation, and the power is concentrated in the karmic cause. Because of this, it has been clearly decided when the reward or retribution will be delivered and in what form. Sometimes, the karmic causes created early in one's life manifest themselves as results in the later years of the same life; other times, they manifest themselves in the next life; and still other times, the things that we create in this life manifest themselves in the life after next.

It is good when we receive the things that we created in this life because we can remember our actions and understand the good and humble reward or retribution that comes our way. However, when karmic retribution has been decided as fixed karma in the next life, the person giving or receiving it has difficulty understanding, and it ends up seeming to be karmic retribution given and received by chance.

I will summarize what I have discussed thus far. If we wonder why it is that the good and evil acts that we perform return to us in the form of a particular reward or retribution, the reason is the presence of the principle of alternating predominance of *yin* and *yang*, which governs the universe and all things. While the creation of karmic retribution is dependent upon the mental and bodily functioning of individuals, it is not the case that retribution appears right away simply because we have used our minds and bodies in a certain way. Rather, it is stored for the time being in the *ālaya* consciousness before eventually returning to us.

# WHEN WE REPENT AND REFORM FOREVER

Ordinary humans and sentient beings live their lives wandering amid a sea of suffering. All of us live in the midst of pain; it is merely a matter of greater and lesser degrees. When a child arrives in this world and is separated from his mother, he encounters a new and unfamiliar environment, and his response is to cry. In essence, this marks his start on the sea of suffering. As we live our lives, there will be pleasant experiences, but a close examination of our life experience shows it to be one of floundering in a sea of suffering.

Even as we grow, we are incapable of satisfying all of the body's desires. When we satisfy a desire, we find ourselves ensnared in even greater punishment and visited by mental anguish. Nor is there any end to our psychological desires for things that we wish to possess. It is very difficult to satisfy such desires. Because of this, we spend a lifetime of eternal desire and dissatisfaction, constantly seeking fulfillment that never arrives.

In addition to this, we sometimes encounter people with whom we exist in a relationship of corresponding harm—we work with them, we live in the same village, or we are part of the same family. The resulting pain is truly great. And this is not all. What about the tremendous torment and pain that we experience when we part with someone whom we have grown to love and care for?

And then there is the truly agonizing pain, the fundamental suffering of aging, sickening, and dying. It comes upon us slowly— the wretchedness of old age, the incapacitation of sickness, the utter inescapability of death. Yet all of us must bow before it. This is the height of suffering in human existence.

These myriad torments do not come very equally to everyone. They visit us in a variety of forms—greater for some, lesser for others. We call these things the natural consequences of our actions. They are not things that others give us; rather, we create them for ourselves.

Unless we awaken with certainty to the principle of the power of karmic action, we will never be free from transgressions and evil. For this reason, we must gain profound knowledge of the Instruction on Repentance.

Ordinary humans do not know the way to escape from a life of transgressions and suffering. Because of this, they either give up and live life as it comes, they repudiate life as painful and sad by its very nature, or they resolve to conquer suffering through their willpower, committing all of their mind and energy to, say, amassing a fortune, seizing privileges, or claiming worldly honors in an all-out bid to escape from suffering.

But as our worldly fortune, honors, and privileges build up and our desires for these things are satisfied, suffering tends to increase even more in proportion to this. This is because we must strive further to preserve them, and we suffer even more greatly when they are compromised. The wise person understands that the more we accumulate, the more we imprison ourselves.

Still, what happens if we possess nothing? We become poor and humble, and endure the suffering of destitution. We suffer when we have, and we suffer when we have not. How are we to live?

When we truly practice repentance, we are able to transcend questions of having and not having and to become free individuals who live their lives commanding such things at will. All of the *Won*-Buddhists who are engaging in this practice now must make clear vows. We must not spend our lives haphazardly patching over the pain of transgressions and suffering or dismissing life as something painful by its nature. Instead, we must find a way of fundamentally overcoming the life of transgression and suffering, and begin a new life. This is why we study the Instruction on Repentance.

As we perform repentance and cultivation of the Way, we must not only wipe away the taint of our transgressive karma from the past and create cleaner good karma, but also achieve liberation even from the good karma and gain a sure understanding of the life of buddhas and bodhisattvas, who command transgressions and blessings as they wish.

# Repentance in Other Religions

When the Buddha, Confucius, Jesus, and the Founding Master came to this world, they regarded it as their primary task and goal to reduce the suffering of sentient beings, and to change the lives of these beings from lives spent agonizing amid transgressions and pain into the lives of buddhas, bodhisattvas, and sages. After arriving on this earth and awakening to the Way, the sages took great pity on the lives of sentient beings and dedicated themselves wholeheartedly to providing succor for the errant lives, exhausting lives, sickened lives, and ignorant lives of sentient beings.

There is an expression, *jesaeng uise*, which means "to deliver all sentient beings from the ocean of misery and cure the world of illness." The sages established their doctrines in order to accomplish this goal. The resulting doctrines are the Four Books and Three Classics of Confucianism, the countless scriptures of Buddhism, the Old and New Testaments in Christianity, and *The Principal Book of Won-Buddhism* and *The Scripture of the Founding Master* in Won-Buddhism. All of these present prescriptions for delivering sentient beings from the ocean of misery and curing the world of illness.

In offering their teachings, however, every one of the sages spoke of repentance for our misdeeds.

The heart of Mahāyāna Buddhism is so-called "self-reliant repentance," in which we focus on washing away the ignorance and karmic obstacles that represent the foundation of transgressive karma, and on recovering our original sinless self-nature.

In contrast, Theravāda Buddhism centers on "dependent repentance," in which we achieve deliverance by confessing our misdeeds before the Three Jewels—the Buddha, the Dharma, and the Sangha—and repenting of them.

One particularly noteworthy example is China's Tiantai School, with its repentance dharmas of *zuo fa, qu xiang,* and *wu sheng.* In *zuo fa* ("make laws") repentance, one seeks to extinguish transgressions by confessing them while making a buddha offering and drawing upon the Buddha's power. In *qu xiang* ("image invoking") repentance, one invokes the marvelous image of buddhas and bodhisattvas wherever one is in order to keep the mind from transgressions. And in *wu sheng* ("without notions") repentance, one seeks to recover the mind that is free of transgressive karma through instruction in the no-mind perspective, allowing one to escape from thoughts of superiority and inferiority, success and failure, and so forth.

Christianity generally uses a method of repentance centered entirely on the power of others, with believers seeking salvation through the grace of Jesus Christ, Mary, and God. While I am not entirely certain of this, the ceremony of baptism in Christianity gives me the impression of the symbolic meaning of using water to wash away transgressive karma. Also, the ritual of confession, in which believers visit a priest to confess their sins, represents another method of repentance. When someone has committed transgressions in his life, he goes to a priest or minister, who represents God and Jesus Christ, confesses all of his offenses, and receives forgiveness for his sins from God. This is an act of repentance and of faith in Christianity.

We, too, can gain psychological comfort and unburden our minds after committing a serious misdeed when we go to a monk, or to our parents, and confess our error, receive admonition, and vow that such a thing will not happen again in the future. It therefore seemed to me that this could represent one method of repentance.

I have discussed the methods of repentance in other religions at a very common-sense level. I hope that you will refer to this as you study how the Founding Master instructed us to engage in repentance practice.

# CHAPTER II

# The Meaning of Repentance

As a rule, "repentance" is the first step in abandoning one's old life and opening oneself to cultivating a new life, and the initial gateway for setting aside unwholesome paths and entering into wholesome paths. For people who repent from past mistakes and continue practicing wholesome paths day by day, past karma will gradually disappear and no karma will be made anew; good paths will come closer day by day and evil paths will recede of their own accord. Therefore, it says in a sūtra, "The mind's previous performance of evil is like a cloud covering the sun; the mind's subsequent generation of good is like the light of a bright lamp dispelling the darkness." Transgressions originally arise from the mind; they perforce will vanish once the mind is extinguished. Karma is originally ignorance; it perforce will vanish in accord with the light of the wisdom of one's self-nature. Those of you who are moaning from the suffering of your transgressions: how can you not enter this gateway?

## Focus on

- How to engage in repentance practice and begin a new life by understanding what repentance is and repenting of our misdeeds, discovering their cause, and remedying it

- How true repentance does not consist of one-time penitence for misdeeds, but repenting of the whole of one's life and entering the life of a buddha and a bodhisattva who do not create transgressive karma

- What exactly is meant by ignorance, the cause of transgression and pain

- How we can extinguish ignorance with the light of the wisdom of our self-nature

# ABANDONING ONE'S OLD LIFE

From the time a person is born and moves beyond his years of infancy, he commences a life of learning in preparation for the existence to come. He goes on to hold various jobs in order to make a living. He forms a family, he pursues spiritual leisure and cultural values, and he lives together with his neighbors and colleagues.

As experiences accumulate with this way of living, they become karma, which will play a crucial part in determining his next life. Thus our way of living is none other than life itself. The life of the sentient being is one of living one way or another according to convention, without any serious concern given to how he should live his life.

For the most part, our lives are a succession of day-to-day routines. Of course, we may occasionally encounter things that go beyond the everyday, but these special events generally cause us tension, and so it is actually easy for us to go about resolving them. In our everyday lives, however, the tension often unravels and our affairs end up in disorder.

In reality, the everyday is what forms the foundation for our life. As a result, when our everyday routine collapses, our life collapses as well, and special ways of life are subject to the influence of our everyday life. The person who is filled with indolence in his everyday life may commit major mistakes due to his indolence, while the person who lives an intemperate life is likely to commit serious misdeeds as a result of that.

Thus we are able to avoid creating transgressive karma and to create good karma according to the amount of fulfillment and value there is in our everyday life, which may be called the foundation of our existence.

## Opening Oneself to Cultivating a New Life

In our everyday life, our surrounding environment and external conditions have a major impact on our way of living. We live in the midst of affairs and affinities that are constantly coming at us on a daily basis. As a result, the way we live is dependent upon our surrounding conditions, and we are unable to live as the actors in our lives. This cannot be called an awakened life, for we are not living on the basis of an acting self. This is generally the approach to life seen among ordinary humans and sentient beings.

In ordinary families, the wife's life is determined by her

husband or children. When the husband disappoints her or the children grow up and leave home, she succumbs to a feeling of emptiness and struggles with despair. The same is true for men: when they live their lives for the sake of achieving glory in the workplace or supporting their children, the time goes by very quickly, and ultimately it is only aging, sickness, and death that await.

The "old life" is a life without agency. Whether we are working for our children, working for our company, or sacrificing ourselves for the sake of the household, our life must be decided and managed by the self as an active agent. The first gateway to repentance consists of abandoning this old life of being controlled by outside conditions, ensuring agency for ourselves, and beginning a new, awakened life.

When we examine our everyday life closely, we see a routine that is repeated daily, as though we are hamsters running on our wheels. Instead of meditating over matters, imagining better values and working to achieve them, we simply repeat a dull and tedious existence filled with routine matters that are the same as they were yesterday and as they will be tomorrow. This continuation leads us to go astray and renders us spiritless, thus constituting the old way of life that causes us to flow along from suffering to suffering and to regress.

We must think about how our final days will unfold if we

continue with what we are doing now. Just as a person may play cards habitually and leave the household in a mountain of debt, so a small bad habit, one that does not seem like much at the beginning, brings tremendous repercussions once repeated and accumulated. We must therefore abandon our old way of living without a plan. We must repent and cultivate a new way of life that has meaning, values, and a plan. If we imbue our everyday life with meaning and value and conduct it according to a plan, it will offer a new way of living in which vitality is with us at all times.

Additionally, most people live their lives in the pursuit of physical health and economic abundance. This is indeed important for our life, but it also tends to turn us into animalistic embodiments of material wealth and to summon forth severe transgressions and evil.

Because of this, those of us whose lives are skewed excessively toward the economic or physical should think deeply and supplement these things with a way of life characterized by clarifying spiritual values and divinity. As is stated in the dharma instruction, this is the way to repent and to cultivate a new way of living.

Going further, we must not restrict our thoughts to this life alone. We must craft a plan for the distant future of eternal life, and we must conduct our todays based on that plan. In their lives, ordinary humans are pressed for time and do not always look far ahead. As a result, they do not live today according to the long view. Instead, they pursue only the immediate reality before them. Thus we must make the transition into living each day without letting the world of truth escape our minds. This will mark the beginning of the life of repentance, in which we abandon our old way of life and cultivate a new one.

# THE INITIAL GATEWAY FOR ENTERING INTO WHOLESOME PATHS

There are countless living creatures in this heaven and earth. There is, of course, the world of the living creatures that we can see, and there is also the world of the living creatures that we cannot see. The number of living creatures truly is too vast to count. We human beings are included among them, and all of you *Won*-Buddhists, and myself, are included among those human beings.

Among these living creatures, there are those with souls that cycle within evil destinies and those with souls that cycle within good destinies. In rare cases, there are also sages who cycle freely among destinies. Repenting is something we do to escape the cycle of good and evil and to live a life of freedom from samsara. It will therefore be easier for us to practice repentance if we have a greater understanding of the lives of living creatures.

This world can be categorized broadly into two worlds: the world of senseless things—heaven, earth, and nature—and the world of sentient beings with souls.

Senseless things do not have a soul within them, and their world centers principally on vital energy. Plants are living and thus have a life force within, but they have no soul that exists independently. Nature and plants are therefore senseless things.

In the world of sentient beings, all of us live our lives with innumerable separately existing souls. This world of the soul is called the "world of the six destinies," as it is divided into six levels. As all of you know, these six worlds of the soul include three in which lives are lived by the soul alone, and three where it lives along with a body, the house of the soul.

## The Worlds of the Six Destinies and Evil Destinies

The three worlds in which the soul alone lives are the worlds of heavenly beings, asuras, and hungry ghosts.

First, there is the world of heavenly beings. This is called the "spirit realm," where beings linger as souls. Those souls that created many blessings or engaged in much mind-practice while living in the human world are able to live in this world of heavenly beings. According to legend, Śākyamuni Buddha also lingered here prior to being born in the world, and arrived in the world of human beings after he took pity on the sentient beings of the *saha* world.

However, because one exists in this world only as a soul, it is impossible to engage actively in the edification of sentient beings, and it is therefore not possible to create blessings. Instead, one spends one's life here spending the blessings one has accumulated. It is also said that, because the environment here is a positive one and so much time is consumed, one does not stay here long—one merely rests here for a brief, set time.

Next, there is the world of the asuras. This is typically called the "world of ghosts." Those who stay in this world have not created enough blessings to receive a body, or they have lost the chance to receive a body because they committed a transgression or had a severe fixation on or rancor toward something. For the most part, living creatures with the habit of roaming from place to place, never staying anywhere for very long, or those who are rash and have the habit of acting and using their minds haphazardly, fail to receive bodies and roam the void as minor demons such as mountain ghosts or ancestral ghosts.

After that, there is the world of hungry ghosts. It is a world of ghosts even humbler than those of the ghost world of asuras. In this lowly ghost world, all manner of animals and denizens of hell roam as souls, unable to receive an appropriate body.

Some of us in Korea, when we go on a picnic, will toss aside a spoonful or two of food before eating. This food is said to be a courtesy for the hungry ghosts that dwell in nearby trees and rocks. People also take care to avoid behaving carelessly with the spirit tree that stands in front of a village because it is said to bring bad luck. The reason, we are told, is that evil spirits live there.

Besides these, there are three worlds in which body and soul exist together: the worlds of human beings, animals, and denizens of hell.

First, there is the world of human beings, which is the selfsame world in which we live. With the human body, there exists a single soul that is proper to this world. This soul is what we call "me," and the agent that controls our body. But because the human body is such a marvel of design and evolution—even more so than the body of an animal—it is said that all living creatures wish to receive a human body.

There is talk about how large the world's population is, but humans are the fewest in number among the six destinies of sentient beings. Only a select few of the countless souls in existence are able to receive a human body. Because of this, receiving a human body is truly a rare occurrence, as well as a wonderful opportunity. Once we have received a human body, we can draw upon its strength to accumulate many merits, and we can engage in practice toward attaining buddhahood.

Next, there is the world of animals. Here, we are typically speaking of beasts: wild animals, mountain animals, fowl, livestock, and so forth. Each of these animals has an individual soul. When we closely observe, say, a bear or a dog, we will see that it has clear idiosyncrasies. The presence of an individual soul means that habits from past lives are manifesting themselves.

Because these animal bodies have capabilities far below those of the human body, any soul that receives an animal body, no matter how outstanding it may be, will inevitably engage in animalistic behavior due to the influence of that body. Most animals will likely be reborn as animals once again. In addition, those who use their bodies in the human world in a squalid manner, fixating solely on instinctual desires, and who cloud the minds of others or commit great transgressions and evil will end up receiving an animal body.

After that, there is hell. The Korean word for "hell," *jiok*, means "earthly prison," and this is literally the case. The insects that roam about under the earth's surface, underwater, and on the ground are all sentient being denizens of hell. Each of them has an individual soul within its body. Once again, it is likely that a denizen of hell will be reborn as another denizen of hell, and it is said that those who commit truly heinous transgressions and evil in their human relationships receive the body of a denizen of hell as retribution for this.

As indicated above, there are boundless numbers of souls within this world of souls. These countless souls do not disappear or emerge out of nowhere; all of them live eternal lives. We use the term "progression" to refer to the souls' movement upward to a worthy world, and the term "regression" to refer to their lingering in a worthless place or moving downward. Depending on how a living creature uses its mind and body, there is a corresponding outcome of progression or regression.

Among these worlds of the six destinies, the one that we most prefer is that of the human being, followed by that of the heavenly being. The latter is the best place of all, but because one only spends blessings there, those who stay there for a long time use up the power of the blessings that they have created and are unable to actively engage in work or practice. Furthermore, it is difficult to create blessings through our affinities. So while we may rest there for a time, it is not a good place to stay for a long time.

The remaining worlds—those of animals, asuras, hungry ghosts, and denizens of hell—are to be avoided. For we cannot engage in mind-practice there, nor can we create blessings, and the environment is such that torment is inevitable. As hungry ghosts and asuras are sometimes spoken of collectively, we speak of the "triple evil world": the worlds of animals, denizens of hell, and hungry ghosts and asuras.

By some stroke of good fortune, we have received human bodies in this lifetime, but it is impossible to guarantee that we will not lapse into the triple evil world in our next life. For this reason, the buddhas and sages of the three periods came, one after the other, to open up the gateway of repentance and let us free ourselves from the cycle through evil destinies.

The true meaning of repentance and cultivation of the Way lies in our reflecting deeply and paying particular attention to our ordinary life and the functioning of our minds so that we might refrain from committing transgressions and evil and instill only good habits, and thereby avoid lapsing into the triple evil world and experiencing suffering.

In their lives, people possess many qualities that could potentially leave them facing the triple evil world. Often, after committing severe transgressions such as harming or killing others, stealing, or engaging in depravities, we become resentful of society and attribute the cause of our transgression to our parents and environment instead of repenting deep in our minds for our misdeeds. This leads us from transgression to transgression, and it is evident that we will cycle into an evil destiny.

But if, after committing a transgression or evil by mistake, out of incorrect thinking, or out of a failure to overcome our desires, we reflect on our error deep in our minds and actively work to avoid transgressing again, this will mark the first step in our leaving behind the unwholesome path and entering the wholesome path.

When people have avoided committing mistakes, they take care not to err. But it is often the case that after making a few mistakes, something of a force of habit builds, and we become repeat offenders. We transgress once again, and we ultimately find ourselves drifting from suffering to suffering in a wretched life of regression. Around us, we often see situations where someone commits an error out of anger or transgresses on the spur of the moment and ultimately ends up wandering in the mire of transgressions and evil. At such times, the way to the wholesome path consists of cultivating a new life on that path by thinking objectively about our future, visiting the temple, and placing deep trust in religious workers.

## Choosing a Profession of Creating Blessings

There are some jobs in which we commit transgressions on a professional basis. Perhaps we are forced to cloud our minds, deceive others, kill living creatures, or organize a house of gambling. When our job becomes a way of making a living and we end up committing countless transgressions and evil as a result, we are obliged to pay for this, and we end up cycling into an evil destiny in which we endure torment as heart-rending as the aggrieved minds of the objects of our deeds.

In selecting a profession, we must make a good choice initially, for we will be doing that work for a long time and our family will be surviving off of it. It is important to have a job that makes others happy, opens up the road for others, respects the public good, and generates wholesome minds.

If, in our ignorance, we made an initial choice of job that forces us to commit transgressions and evil, it will not be easy to change, for people have to earn a living. But if we understand that we commit transgressions and evil because of our jobs, and that we and the family members whom we love suffer from lapsing into the triple evil world as a result, we will have to make the effort to change jobs. We must accept the suffering of eating less and spending less and seek out new employment. We need to ensure that our earnings are fair, that we act in accordance with the wishes of others, and that we perform corresponding good actions with part of our earnings.

I once heard about the travails of an obstetrician, who explained that the doctors at the clinic sometimes killed embryos. If you listen to someone who has worked slaughtering cattle, he will tell you that the look in the cow's eye as it is dragged off to die is so plaintive that he cannot bear it. As a result, he may drink, or he may have others do the work of taking the cow away.

How unfortunate it is for our eternal life if our working life becomes one where we are forced to commit transgressions and evil. Repentance and cultivation of the Way mean leaving behind unwholesome paths and proceeding toward a wholesome one by reflecting deeply upon our professional life.

# Transgressive Pastimes

It is truly sad to watch someone who enjoys fishing. Likewise, the heart aches to see someone encourage gambling. It is not difficult to find examples around us of people who use drugs or commit transgressions and evil through their hobbies rather than their jobs.

How foolish and ignorant of the truth our life is when this precious existence becomes interspersed with enjoyments that involve the commission of transgressions. The path of repentance is one of reflecting upon this, changing course, and boldly substituting these practices with lifegiving and wholesome hobbies.

We must recognize that the path of transgressions and evil is one where, due to a paralyzed consciousness or lack of discriminative ability, we fail to understand what is a transgression and what is a blessing, basing our thinking instead on the fashions of the world at large and the people around us. Furthermore, we must have faith that we who have committed transgressions will be punished, and we must put this belief into practice. This is the shortcut from the unwholesome path to the wholesome one.

Also, we must understand that the way from the unwholesome path to the wholesome path involves befriending and interacting with people who respect morals and ethics, and changing ours to a life in which we stay close to the pious atmosphere of illuminating cause and effect and serving the truth, in the presence of psychological stability and teachers who help us to refrain from self-indulgence.

If we boldly cast aside our old daily life—a life ensnared in the ignorance and karmic obstacles of creating transgressive karma—and the life of cycling into evil destinies, in which we lapse into the suffering of samsara and commit grave transgressions, and we practice instead a life of accumulating good works and cultivating the wholesome path to liberation from samsara, the cycling past karma will gradually diminish, and our new karma will be good karma. Thus all of us must achieve enlightenment and awakening and proceed on the path of repentance and cultivation of the Way.

# TRANSGRESSIONS ORIGINALLY ARISE FROM THE MIND

Transgression is the enemy of humankind and living creatures and the thing that they should fear the most. It binds us and condemns us to agony. Transgression is something unacceptable, something that destroys the social order, threatens human survival, diminishes quality of life, and shrouds us in anxiety and exhaustion.

This is why all of the buddhas and sages of the past, present, and future came to this world and provided a guiding hand of salvation, so that all living creatures might escape from the abyss of transgression and evil; why they established means of deliverance, forming religions and providing teachings; and why they have inspired religious workers to realize a world that is free of transgression.

The Chinese character for "transgression" (罪) is a pictograph that shows a "not" (非) trapped in a "net" (罓). This means that when we do something bad, we are caught in the net of law, trapped behind the bars of the conscience.

Over the course of their life together in families or in the community of a society, humans make a shared social commitment to protect and advance that society, the family, and human beings in general. We can call this "the law." And as humans have lived over the ages, they have also followed a moral code, an ethical consciousness, telling them how they should use their minds and behave. This represents the traditional conventions of that society, as well as its culture. Transgression is the act of defying and disregarding these laws, morals, and ethics.

The buddhas and sages of the three periods awakened to the principle of the universe and, based on this realization, learned what way of human life is most suited to that principle, what method of conducting human relationships is suited to the truth, and by what principles societies, states, and the world should operate to conform to the truth. They turned this knowledge into doctrine and spread it throughout their society, where it became the conscience of each individual, the standard for determining right and wrong, and the ethical norm of that society. Transgression is when we defy, disregard, or mistake these words of the sages.

In particular, all of the sages established precepts and instructed sentient beings to abide by them without fail, thus preventing transgressions from occurring or enabling people to avoid committing transgressions directly. These precepts can be explained in terms of two main types of character. In one, it is a transgression to violate the precepts themselves—for example, with murder or thievery. In the other, it is not a crime per se to fail to abide by the precepts, but doing so serves to call forth transgressive karma. This may include drinking alcohol or dressing in an ostentatious way. As such, violation of the precepts inevitably entails transgressions and evil.

Upon the foundation of shared commitments or cultural practices of humankind and the words of the sages, the state establishes laws and instructs people to obey them. It is transgression to defy these laws, and, if we go a bit deeper, it is transgression to defy the conscience and morals prescribed by the sages.

What is important here is that because there are so many instances in which people cannily evade social laws and commit crimes, when people are led to repent merely through social laws, unseen transgressions and evil take root within that society, causing it to collapse internally and wreaking devastation upon human lives.

While it is important to monitor the members of a society externally so that they do not commit transgression, religion must come ahead of this, so that all people profoundly understand the essence of transgression, awaken to and realize the fear of transgressive karma, and live a life of truly avoiding the commission of transgressions.

There is another saying: "Ten people cannot watch a single thief." There are limits to monitoring social thievery through surveillance. The problem is that the individual and the society will only be delivered and prosper together when each individual understands the essence of morality and dedicates his mind and energies to upholding it.

## Ignorance Is the Foundation of Transgression and Evil

Christianity tells of the original sin. Adam and Eve were the progenitors of humankind. Adam was the husband, Eve the wife, and the two of them lived together in the Garden of Eden through the providence of God. In the garden was the very appetizing fruit of the Tree of the Knowledge of Good and Evil. God delivered a precept to Adam and Eve commanding that they not eat of this fruit. But then Satan came and tempted Eve into taking a bite. After eating the apple, Adam and Eve came to know shame, and practices such as discrimination between men and women emerged. Christianity teaches that the original sin of humankind was the act of eating the fruit of the Tree of the Knowledge of

Good and Evil in defiance of God's instruction not to do so. As a result, the sin of Adam and Eve, the progenitors of humankind, was carried down to future generations, and for this reason all humans today are sinners. Of course, this is a story, and so we should not be concerned with its rationality or factuality.

Looking at it closely, we see that their sin was to disobey the word of God. If the law tells us to do certain things and not to do certain other things, then it is transgression to defy it. It is worth noting that because it is a sin to defy the word of God, this also means that a Christian who hopes to avoid sinning is free of sin as long as he obeys and does not defy the word of God.

What of Confucianism, which has had such a tremendous impact on Eastern society? What does it view as the essence of transgression? Confucianism tells us that humans have within them a heaven-like mind, the fundamental nature. This fundamental mind is the heaven mind, free of transgression, but because it is obscured by the physical nature—human feeling— various transgressions and evil emerge from it. Thus it is said that the transgression begins when the human mind obscures the heaven mind.

In our religions of Buddhism and Won-Buddhism, the Dharmakāya Buddha truth—that is, the Il-Won-Sang Truth—is the principle that forms the nature of the human being and, further, is present in all things. Failure to understand even that principle is called "ignorance." This ignorance—that is, ignorance of the truth—is the nursery for the commission of all transgressions, and lack of understanding is said to be the state of transgression and evil.

The Founding Master also told us that the truth, broadly speaking, gave us the Grace of Heaven and Earth through heaven and earth, the Grace of Parents through our parents, the Grace of Fellow Beings through our fellow beings, and the Grace of Laws through laws. He said that by lacking awareness of this grace, we commit the transgression of ingratitude. In other words, he viewed ignorance of the graces as a fundamental cause of transgression.

Thus far, I have talked about the concepts of transgression in various religions. They do share common aspects on the whole, but they give the impression of expressing their concepts with different focuses due to their respective cultural backgrounds.

However, if we take the view that, in terms of human psychology, one can obey the commands of God if one has awakened with certainty to the will of Heaven, and one can stave off the perverse desires of the human mind if one has awakened to and understood the heaven mind of the fundamental nature, then it seems that the more primeval teaching is that it is transgression to be ignorant of the buddha dharma principle of non-arising, non-ceasing, and retribution and response of cause and effect, and the fundamental grace that we have received from the Dharmakāya

Buddha Il-Won-Sang.

In summary, it may be said that transgression is ignorance—namely, ignorance of the truth—and arises out of that ignorance.

In the Instruction, the Founding Master tells us that "transgressions originally arise from the mind." I will now explain in a bit more detail about the pathway by which transgressions arise from the mind.

When our mind is in a state of no-mind, there is no transgression. When ours is the original pure mind, the tranquil mind, there is no state of transgression and evil. This mind is called the mind of the void and calm, numinous awareness, and the state of the ever-calm, ever-alert mind that is tranquil and clear.

This original mind encounters sensory conditions. The conditions of the six perceptions—what is seen, heard, smelled, tasted, touched, or thought—appear through the six sense organs. It is as though a guest suddenly arrives in a quiet and peaceful home. These conditions may be beneficial to us, or they may be useless or harmful.

If, when our minds perceive such conditions, we either do not accept them or do not produce the mind to hate, resent, kill, or deceive the object even in the case of bad conditions, then this is not transgression. But if the desire to possess is activated and we generate a mind of greed, anger, or the intent to deceive, which leads us to cause direct harm to others, harbor the mind to do so, or plot a crime, then this is transgression.

In order to prevent the committing of such transgressions, a religion (or what have you) sets precepts and demands that we abide by them rigorously. Thus it is a transgression when, after we encounter an external condition, a mind of greed, anger, or delusion is activated within us and we violate a precept or law that must not be violated.

For instance, imagine that a guest comes calling from outside with some business, which he proposes going in on together. The wise owner of the house forms the prior judgment that the action would be wrong, and he tells the guest that he cannot work with him, providing legitimate reasons for this and sending him on his way. Surely, this cannot be a transgression. He has prevented a transgression from occurring because he had a mind of wisdom rather than one of ignorance of the truth. However, what if the owner had taken up the guest's suggestion, agreed to participate in this bad action, and conspired to bring it to fruition? That would be transgression.

So even if sensory conditions of greed, anger, or delusion arrive from outside, we can always avoid committing transgressions if we preserve a mind that is aware of the truth—our ever-calm, ever-alert mind that is originally free of transgression—and if we possess a mind that is awakened to the cause and effect that transforms objects.

Ultimately, all transgression originates in ignorance of the truth. What we must be wary of here, however, is that if, despite having the awareness to make the judgment that the guest's intentions are bad, we fail to eliminate the desire that arises within or we succumb to the guest's suasions, our knowledge will be no great source of strength to us. In addition to precisely determining the guest's intentions, we also need the strength of cultivation to eliminate the desires that arise within and to avoid being swayed by the guest's temptation.

In the Instruction, we are told that transgressions "perforce will vanish once the mind is extinguished." As explained before, even if desire begins to operate internally as the six sensory organs of the eyes, ears, nose, tongue, body, and mind encounter the six perceptions of the seen, heard, smelled, tasted, touched, and known, and we are tempted by the external conditions, the transgressing mind will vanish when we dissolve the mind of transgression and evil by engaging in practice to guide that mind and assess it against the original mind.

All of us have most likely had experiences with how a mind can be extinguished. We arouse a mind toward something, only to gather it back in and eliminate it if our plans seem unlikely to work out. Thus the mind-practice of producing and eliminating a mind is of crucial importance when engaging in repentance practice.

We open and close doors dozens of times each day. Recently, we have come to see doors that open automatically and those that open by hand, but the mind is similar from the perspective of giving forth and gathering back. Minds arise and vanish tens of thousands of times each day.

Sometimes, a mind arises and embeds itself firmly at the bottom of one's mind. We call this type of mind the "attachment mind." Other minds arise and hide away deep in our mind-pocket, from which they make their presence known from time to time. Still others arise only to vanish right away, leaving us unable to even remember them.

When such minds come and go, we must clear away those that summon forth transgression and those that have no meaning. If we allow these minds to linger for a long time, they can generate similar ones, which obscure our radiant minds and cause clouded judgment. Because of this, we must practice extinguishing these defilements and idle thoughts by illuminating them with the light of the mind.

Also, we must ensure that good minds, minds that bring blessings, are in place to be put into action later on. These include legitimate wishes, the mind of faith, the practicing mind, the mind of charitable acts, and the spirit of self-sacrifice.

Yet there are also times when these good minds actually obscure the path before us. Sometimes, they may cloud our spirit and cause us to commit transgressions. For instance, we may enjoy the spirit of the public good and create good karma through actions that contribute to that good. But when we see someone who does not possess that spirit, there arises in us a mind to disregard or despise him, and so we transgress—by criticizing him, by humiliating him in front of others, and so forth. Likewise, when other people are unaware of their good minds, or when they engage in actions that go against them, such a mind can arouse in us a mind of transgression and evil. For this reason, even such a good mind must be ministered to well if it is not to become a mind of transgression for us.

Sometimes, a person commits some small misdeed and is unable to rid himself of that consciousness of transgression. He may become consumed by a sense of inferiority, and his personality may change to become very passive as a result, or he may abandon himself to reckless behavior and commit great transgressions. He may even commit suicide. It is a good mind that recognizes misdeeds, but at times that mind can go too far and actually create transgressions.

Today, we frequently see cases where people engage in wars because of religion. These people tell each other that their battles are a "holy war." But because this is based on the standard of their own good minds, and they view others who are not the same way as immoral people, their sense of righteousness leads to war and ultimately to the commission of enormous transgressions and evil. Even if we possess a good mind by our own standards, we must not let our minds be darkened by that mind so that we commit errors in our judgments of universal principles and human affairs.

# WHAT IS KARMA?

There are some people who ask, "What need have we for religion? Can't we simply live according to the law with a good heart?" We also speak of people who are so kind that they need no laws to live a good life. But even those people who live with good hearts and do many good things for others may be visited by some unknowable destiny and encounter misfortune. Due to our mistaken judgment of principles and affairs, we may seek to do good things only to end up enabling bad things to occur. Sometimes, the thing we do for the sake of another ultimately brings him harm.

When we look into the pure and innocent face of a child, we cannot see even the shadow of transgression and evil. Yet even many of these innocent children are visited by illness and lose their lives, while others meet with sudden accidents and are left crippled.

Life is not so simple that it is enough merely to do good

deeds. When unforeseen misfortune comes upon us, we lament it to ourselves, wondering what karmic retribution we created in previous lives that such suffering is visiting us now. Why do such sinless children and virtuous people find themselves experiencing sudden misfortune?

It is all because of karmic retribution that we created in previous lives and are receiving in turn in this one. Such retribution visits us under the name of "chance" and "destiny." It binds us with its ropes so that we are never free. For this reason, the person engaged in repentance practice must have a profound understanding of this karmic retribution.

## There Exists a Thing Called Karmic Retribution

Karma is a word that comes from Sanskrit. It describes a sleeping force, a hidden force gathering strength, one that does not manifest its power immediately but is capable of operating at some future time. For this reason, it is also called "dormant power."

Let us look at an example. When the people in this world who bear responsibility for governance make repeated mistakes, the ones who suffer as a result of them carry their discontentment in their minds without giving it expression. If there are many mistakes in many different areas, the hidden resentments will build up in each of those places. The states thus accumulated are called "social karma," and when something triggers their sudden outpouring, they show an enormous power—depending on the circumstances, they may well provide the driving force behind social upheavals.

In the same way, the results of our use of body and mind cluster together in a hidden place. This place is called the "storehouse consciousness." In Sanskrit, it is referred to as the *ālaya-vijñāna*; we sometimes call it a "karma pocket." In it, all manner of good and bad karma is stored up like so many seeds.

When a plane crash occurs, the investigators locate the black box and analyze its contents to determine the cause of the accident. In this case, it could be said that the black box is like the storehouse consciousness, and its contents are like the power of karmic action.

All of you here have a karma pocket within your mind, a kind of black box. And that karma pocket stores all of the actions of your body and mind. But when information is stored in a black box, it is said, a time is scheduled for those karma seeds to sprout and produce some outcome. Broadly speaking, karmic retribution is stored in two ways.

One of these is storage in the so-called "self-caused room," which contains the habits we have instilled in ourselves. In the main, this storehouse holds gifts that we have instilled in ourselves. The person who practices calligraphy stores up the seeds of penmanship skills, the person who exercises a lot stores up the seeds of athletic talent, the person with finely honed skills stores up the seeds of that workmanship, and the person who sings many songs stores up the seeds of singing talent. Likewise, the person who frequently deceives others with falsehoods stores up a talent for fraud.

We also store the seeds of personality characteristics in our self-caused room according to how frequently we have applied a certain personality in our daily life. Similarly, we create and store all manner of seeds for habits of the mind, habits of speech, and habits of the body through the actions we take in accordance with our determinations, through our words, and through our behavior with our bodies.

During my time at the Central Headquarters, children would come every spring to play and draw pictures. One day, I saw two children with crayons drawing Song Dae, the House of Pine. I looked closer and saw that while the two of them were drawing the same object, one was using dark colors and the other light and cheerful colors. As a result, the first child's picture looked dreary and depressing, while the second child's picture looked light and carefree. I asked them why they had used those colors, and they told me that it was just the way they drew them.

Even when we are drawing pictures, the colors that we prefer are stored up in our self-caused room before manifesting themselves. The colors and patterns of the clothes that all of you are wearing right now are, to a large extent, an expression of the self-caused karma you have stored in your self-caused room. The seeds planted in this room are manifested as our character and other traits in the next life according to their personality. The content of our self-caused room becomes our karma.

There is also an "other-caused room." On the other side of our karma pocket, we store the content of what we have experienced at the hands of other living creatures and the relationships that we have formed with one another. When another person does a kindness for me, a sense of profound gratitude toward him arises in my mind, and a seed of grace toward him is stored up in my other-caused room. If I receive favors from him for many years, even more seeds of grace are stored to eventually sprout at a later time; I will repay him with a mind of great happiness, performing services for him or sharing with him the things I possess.

I am sure that all of you have had such an experience, of having the desire to give to someone and doing things for him even though you were not receiving any help from him at the time. Conversely, when someone does us harm, we feel discontentment in our minds after being forced to sustain the damage, and we develop a mind of resentment. In this case, those feelings turn into seeds of harm toward that person and are stored away in the other-caused room within our karma pocket. If you encounter that person in your next lives, you will exact repayment from the object of your resentment, even if he is someone whom everyone else praises as a wonderful person, and you alone are doing him harm.

Over the course of our countless lifetimes, we form relationships, both good and bad, with other living creatures and store various kinds of karma within each other's karma pockets. There are relationships of corresponding lifegiving, where the two parties only plant good things and exchange grace with each other, and there are relationships of corresponding harm, where the two parties preserve each other's seeds of bad karma before eventually retaliating against one another.

No matter how good a relationship may be, it is difficult to sow only good karma seeds with one another at all times. Because of this, we sometimes sow bad karma seeds along with the good and good seeds along with the bad, leading to human relationships where seeds of hatred and love intermingle in a complex mixture.

In every case, we create good and bad with one another and store up what we are to receive in the future in that person's other-caused room. Sometimes, we store up blessings there to receive them in kind eventually, and sometimes we store up harm there and receive that in kind.

## Karma Is Originally Ignorance

Thus far, I have been talking about good and bad karma. My goal in so doing is to interpret the words of the Instruction on Repentance, which says, "karma is originally ignorance." Previously, I noted that karma includes, first, the karma of good and bad habits that we create and store up ourselves, and, second, the good and bad karma that becomes formed, and must be repaid, within a relationship of give and take with another person.

In this way, all karma is the result of what is stored up through our mental and bodily functioning. It gathers together as seeds and builds up a force that is paid back as grace or as harm when we encounter our counterpart. For this reason, this force contained within karma is called the "power of karmic action."

As an example, when we encounter someone whom we hate, a powerful mind of hatred and retaliation surges up from somewhere deep in our minds. It is a force beyond our control. Likewise, the loving mind, which emanates from the deepest reaches of our minds, operates with a fearsome force and is thus difficult for us to restrain.

When karma gathers into karmic power in this way, we act according to its dictates; its power leaves us no opportunity to examine the context. Karmic force also obscures our minds, and this darkness becomes an obstacle that blocks our path forward. For this reason, it is called a "karmic obstacle."

Because of this, the words "Karma is originally ignorance" should be understood to mean less that karma itself is ignorance, and more that karmic obstacles arise due to the power of karmic action and obscure the path before us.

With regard to the use of the word "ignorance," I mentioned before that ignorance occurs because karma has brought darkness upon us, but in another sense the word is used to mean bringing about transgression in terms of one's whole existence due to the delusion caused by failure to understand the truth. I hope there will be no misunderstanding about this.

I have an acquaintance who failed the civil service examination a number of times. In the end, he gave up taking the test and went to work as a junior official at a rural government office. While he was studying for the examination, he had a girlfriend whom he loved dearly. Her treatment of him was so good, he said, that the feeling of love left him unable to devote himself wholeheartedly to his studies. He sometimes laments today that he might have passed the examination when he was younger were it not for this woman, who is now his wife.

These two people planted seeds of grace within each other in past lives. They met in this life, and so strong was the power of affection from that hidden grace that they could not control it, with the result that it ultimately obscured the path ahead of them. Even though the karma was good, there was no dharma power to control the tempo, and it consequently turned into a karmic obstacle of ignorance.

Thus good or bad karma does not become ignorance in and of itself. Rather, the person who is not yet proficient with his practice is unable to control its power, and it obscures his wisdom and clouds his judgment, leading to ignorance.

## Dissolving Karmic Power with the Light of the Wisdom of One's Self-Nature

The Instruction on Repentance tells us, "Karma is originally ignorance; it perforce will vanish in accord with the light of the wisdom of one's self-nature." Every religion makes different claims about how to go about dissolving the karmic obstacles blocking one's path.

Western religions primarily emphasize the power of others. It is taught that if one prays earnestly, God will extinguish the transgressive karma created by a sentient being through His absolute authority. Thus it is believed that the agent in one's salvation is not oneself—salvation is only possible through a god or savior.

In Theravāda, or Southern, Buddhism, it is believed that transgressive karma is created by the person, but that salvation comes in the form of deliverance by the dharma-power of the Buddha or by Avalokiteśvara, Kṣitigarbha, or Amitābha.

But it cannot be said that this idea—that some other person completely eliminates for us the karmic obstacles that we have created ourselves—constitutes a complete teaching. At first, we may indeed draw upon the strength of others, through faith or through the power of prayer, obtaining comfort in our minds and solace for the pain of transgressive karma. But no other person can receive the transgressive karma that we have created for ourselves, and so it is impossible for transgressive karma to be totally extinguished through some outside power. We must unravel the knots we tie ourselves. Complete salvation is ultimately something that we must undertake on our own.

Extinguishing karmic obstacles with the wisdom of the light of one's self-nature means that because we have a Dharmakāya Buddha present within our mind, it is possible for us to escape the darkness of karmic obstacles with the wisdom-light of the self-nature buddha that is harbored within ourselves.

All of us have a self-nature buddha that is just like a buddha within us. It is called "the void and calm, numinous awareness." The self-nature buddha is utterly empty and tranquil, and it possesses a marvelous light. We call this the "fundamental wisdom," or "*prajñā* wisdom."

When a practitioner engages in profound mind-practice and

comes to understand the self-nature buddha, a limitless light of wisdom surges forth. With this, he is able to dissolve any karmic obstacles that come his way by shining the light of the wisdom of his self-nature upon them. Just as darkness is naturally dispelled when we shine a bright light upon a dark place, so any karmic obstacles that come upon us are extinguished when we shine the bright light of the self-nature upon them. This process of dissolving karmic obstacles is called "reflecting the light inward on the original nature."

When karmic obstacles of defilements and idle thoughts arise, the ordinary person is besieged by these obstacles on all sides, going from transgression to transgression as his karmic power dictates. But buddhas and bodhisattvas use the light of self-nature to dissolve the obstacles and return to a clean mind. When we ride an airplane as it soars up off the ground and through the clouds, all we see around us is blue sky. So it is with liberation from karmic obstacles. From this point forward, I will explain in a bit more detail when speaking of the methods of repentance.

# CHAPTER III

# Incorrect Repentance

However, the foundations of transgressive karma are greed, hatred, and delusion. No matter how repentant you may be, if you subsequently repeat an evil action, there will never be a day when transgressions are extinguished. Furthermore, even though people who have committed serious transgressions and fall into the evil destinies may accumulate a certain amount of merit through temporary repentance, their transgressions will remain as such even while they receive merit according to their meritorious actions, so long as they leave the original greed, hatred, and delusion intact. This is like someone who tries to cool down the water boiling in a large cauldron by pouring a little bit of cold water on top while letting the fire underneath continue to burn: the strength of the fire is strong while that of the cold water is weak, so the water will never cool down.

There are many people in the world who repent of their previous mistakes, but few who do not repeat those mistakes subsequently. Some people perform one or two types of merit through a temporary sense of repentance, but leave the greed, hatred, and delusion intact in their own minds; how can such persons hope to have their transgressive karma purified?…

Recently there have been groups of self-styled enlightened ones occasionally appearing who, making light of the precepts and discipline and of cause and effect, have acted as they pleased and stopped as they pleased under the guise of "unconstrained action," thus sullying in some cases the gateway of the buddha. This occurs because they realize only that the self-nature is free from discrimination, but do not realize that it also involves discriminations; how can this be knowing the true Way that transcends being and nonbeing? Furthermore, there are many people who think they have completed their practice just by seeing the nature and have no use for repentance or practice after seeing the nature. Even if seeing the nature has occurred, the myriad of defilements and all attachments are not simultaneously annihilated and, even if one has gained the three great powers and achieved buddhahood, one cannot avoid one's own fixed karma. One must pay close attention to this point and avoid falling into perverted views or making light of transgressive karma by misinterpreting the words of the buddhas and enlightened masters.

## Focus on

- The identity of the greed, hatred, and delusion that are the fundamental causes behind the creation of transgressive karma

- What temporary repentance is

- What we must do to avoid committing subsequent mistakes

- What constitute mistaken approaches to repentance, such as engaging in "unconstrained action" and committing transgressions simply because one has seen the nature

# THE FOUNDATIONS OF TRANSGRESSIVE KARMA ARE GREED, HATRED, AND DELUSION

Previously, I provided an explanation on what transgression is. It refers to mental and bodily functioning that blocks the path ahead of us, or mistaken actions that cause harm to others either directly or indirectly. Karma, in turn, refers to the storage of the transgressions that we commit so that we receive corresponding punishment later, as well as of the good deeds that we do, with the resulting happiness stored up in our *ālaya* consciousness.

The most fundamental cause of transgressive karma is ignorance. Ignorance means a lack of awareness of the truth. More concretely, it means being unaware of the principle whereby we receive punishment when we commit a wicked transgression and we receive a reward from the truth when we perform good actions.

What exists to ensure that we are rewarded or punished correspondingly when we commit good or bad deeds? As explained previously, there exists in this universe a principle of alternating predominance of *yin* and *yang*, and we are rewarded and punished as a result of this principle.

Ignorance means being unaware of the truth that governs this universe and every one of the individual beings that dwell within it. It is because of this ignorance that we form mistaken judgments from our experiences and perform mistaken actions, and thus come to commit transgressions and evil.

However, it cannot be said that ignorance of the truth is punished immediately. There are many chances for ignorance to lead us to commit transgressions and evil, but we cannot declare that all actions taken in ignorance are transgressions and evil, just as it is not the case that a person's every action is a crime simply because he is unaware of the laws of his country. When we are ignorant of the law, we are liable to commit a crime, but this does not mean that all of our actions are crimes.

Ultimately, ignorance provides the foundation for the commission of transgressions and evil. This ignorance, or the karmic power built up from the past, serves as a cause, while the direct cause of the commission of transgressions and evil lies in the three poison minds of greed, hatred, and delusion. For this reason, the Founding Master said that greed, hatred, and delusion are the foundations of transgressive karma.

All humans have the desire to possess. When that desire is excessive, the mind of greed begins to operate. Because of this mind, we hate others, we spend sleepless nights, we suffer all manner of disease, the causes of social conflict arise, our minds lose their equilibrium, and our judgment of good and evil becomes clouded, leading us to commit transgressions and evil.

To explain this mind of greed in slightly more detail, it consists of physical desire, desire for fortune, desire for honors, desire for food, and desire for greater comfort. As these desires develop, they lead to the desire to protect one's family and, further, the desire to protect one's causal affinities, the intellectual desire to carry one's claims, and so forth. These desires know no end, and when they are not fulfilled we experience hatred: a fiery rage erupts within us and we commit acts of brutality. When anger is not simply produced within our minds but is expressed through evil language or acts of violence, this constitutes transgressions and evil. Perhaps, we will keep ourselves farther away from transgressions and evil if we are able to gain the ability to freely control this angry mind.

Some people become angry when they are unable to satisfy their greed, and some tell lies and engage in trickery. The wicked mind, the petty schemer, the swindler—all of them suffer the mind of delusion. This delusion is the culprit behind the commission of transgressions and evil. The mind of delusion has painted a coat of lies over the true mind, the pure mind. Those who have that mind deceive their own original mind and deceive others with false expressions on their face, false words, and false writing, using them as a means of satisfying their own greed.

Even so, it is still pure for us to reveal our greed directly. If it is innocent transgression and evil to rise to anger when our greed is not satisfied, the root of an even deeper evil is the false mind, the scheming mind—in other words, the mind of delusion.

Sometimes, we find ourselves taken in by this mind of delusion. We often see examples of people who deceive the public in the name of justice. Often, the person himself has been taken in by his own justification. When we are not capable of examining our minds closely, we frequently end up deceived by the false mind ourselves, and commit transgressions and evil as a result.

When our repentance is not true, it is because we are unaware of, and under the command of, the greed, hatred, and delusion that are the direct causes of transgressions and evil. It may be that we are aware of them yet still unable to overcome the three poison minds.

# Temporary Repentance

People live their lives carrying in their mind a bundle of transgressions and evil that they have the potential to commit. Just as we can observe the afflicted area in someone who is suffering from a malignant tumor, locating the roots at the foundation of that tumor within its suppuration, so too do the three poison minds of greed, hatred, and delusion form the foundation within our minds for committing transgressions and evil. If we are unable to remove the greed, hatred, and delusion that form the roots of transgressions and evil, we will ultimately find ourselves committing transgressions. Even if we repent, we will continue to commit further transgressions, living within a constant flux of transgression.

It is easy for us to commit transgressions, but the pain of punishment is torturous. Young people in their adolescent years have desires that are difficult to curb, but if they cannot control these desires, their commission of transgressions, however momentary they may be, may result in a punishment that is extremely harsh and enduring.

When we think only of this life and remain unaware of the principle by which we receive in the next lives as we have created in this one, we commit transgressions without much of a sense of fear. We must break free from the deluded belief that the mistakes of our past simply fade away with the passage of time. The past that has gone by returns to us in the form of our future. When we understand the principle by which we receive as we have created, when we have a clear understanding of past, present, and future lives, perhaps then we will seldom commit transgressions.

The person who lives his life going from hardship to hardship is liable to succumb to resignation. When this happens, he is prone to committing major transgressions. The person who loves his life, embracing and taking responsibility for all things he does, good and evil alike, will seldom commit transgressions.

Objects operate according to the law of inertia. Similarly, we humans also find it comfortable to repeat today what we did yesterday. We call this "habit." Good habits build an outstanding character and a life of creating blessings, but bad habits cause harm to society and cause ourselves to succumb to the morass of corruption.

When someone commits one or two mistakes, we tend to be generous and forgive him. But if he continues committing one mistake after another, he is unlikely to be forgiven. The bad habit of regretting our mistakes only to repeat them once again brings about major transgressions and evil and causes us to cycle eternally through evil destinies.

All around us, we see people who travel in and out of police stations and prisons as though these were their homes. We see people whose neighbors call them "thugs," "gamblers," "swindlers," "drug addicts," and "foul-mouthed." Clearly, this is not how they were to begin with. In all likelihood, they engaged in such actions one or two times, and those actions subsequently turned into a habit, gaining more and more momentum until, before they knew it, these people had become so-called "producers of transgression and evil."

Countless blessings return to the person who does good, and countless traps await the person who does evil, preventing him from being free and causing him to travel from torment to torment.

I remember one year when the Seoul Service Association held a bazaar. With the proceeds, we visited a welfare facility for the mentally disabled. We delivered donations, and we also did laundry and bathed the patients. At the time, we had a true sense of what a severe karmic retribution they were receiving—having a low mental age and being unable to use body and mind as they wished. A fellow *Won*-Buddhist who went with us at the time recounted having profound awakenings after seeing people who had received human bodies yet were not whole, whose minds were incomplete.

Having a profession that clouds the minds of others, engaging in affairs that obstruct the path before others, disrupting the social good by living an animalistic life or harming virtuous groups, abusing power to inflict great harm on the masses—when we habitually repeat such transgressions, the road before us will be an indescribable continuation of misfortune.

One time, I visited a facility that housed people who were suffering from Hansen's disease (leprosy). Even here, there were people who had been incarcerated in a detention facility for committing crimes. The experience left me with emotions of great pity in my mind. The people who had contracted Hansen's disease were fearsome enough, but it was truly heartbreaking to see that some of them were confined to life in prison for committing further misdeeds.

Among the illustrative stories frequently told by the Founding Master, there is one about a person suffering from Hansen's disease. An old monk and a young monk went on a walk at what is today Naeso Temple on Mt. Byeonsan. It was the spring, and the old monk saw a slash-and-burn farmer setting fire to the mountain to clear a field. "Do you see that young farmer clearing a field over there?" he asked. "One day, he will grow old and become a leper. Every year, when he sets fire to clear a field, many living creatures will die in the blaze, and they will come back as leprosy bacteria that will torment him. Mark this well, and come back some day. You will see." The old monk later died, and the young monk grew old himself. One day, he was walking near the temple and saw a leper looking at the forest ahead and lamenting, "Now I have leprosy and can no longer clear the field." The monk inquired and found that it was the same slash-and-burn farmer who had cleared that field many years before.

We must have a clear understanding that the cause of all disease, all torment, all social censure, is karmic retribution for transgressions committed with or without our knowledge. All living creatures live amid an abundance of karmic retribution for things they have done both knowingly and unknowingly from their past lives until today, and they receive that retribution over the course of their lives. At the same time, some of them engage in repentance that is not true but superficial, temporary, lacking an understanding of principles. While this may be better than no repentance at all, one cannot be free forever from transgression and evil this way. We must therefore learn how to engage in sincere and eternal repentance.

# MISUNDERSTANDING
# UNCONSTRAINED ACTION

Up to this point, I have referred to the mistake of repentance without knowledge of principles, temporary repentance, and repentance without gaining control over habit. Now, I will focus on explaining the words from the latter part of the Instruction on Repentance: "Recently there have been groups of self-styled enlightened ones occasionally appearing . . . . One must . . . avoid . . . making light of transgressive karma by misinterpreting the words of the buddhas and enlightened masters."

These words point reproachfully to the fact that certain practitioners neglect their repentance practice once they have gained some degree of understanding and a small amount of ability from a little practice. It seems that it would be expedient to include this in the section on "Incorrect Repentance," so I will explain here in a bit more detail.

When we awaken to practice and engage in exertion and the accumulation of merits, strength builds up in our minds, and we may develop the feeling that we can move the whole world, or the temporary sense that there is no obstruction in anything we do.

In such cases, it is all the more crucial that we receive with humble mind the particular guidance of a teacher, and that we spur on our efforts toward exertion and the accumulation of merits, engaging in character training that follows in line with the dharma and becoming people who are socially recognized. Yet some practitioners place their faith in some slight, temporary strength and talk of "unconstrained action"—showing a disregard for precepts and for cause and effect and neglecting to develop a socially objectivized character, and ultimately fail at the great Way and stray along their path.

When ordinary humans and sentient beings repent deeply for their transgressive karma and engage in the fervent practice of faith, they arrive at a stage where they begin practice with a sense awakened in them that they, too, must engage in mind-practice. This could be called the first steps of mind-practice; there, we continue accumulating merits, and a bit of strength gathers in the mind. In the process, we may encounter a very dangerous stage in which our minds begin to look infinitely large, the world rather small in comparison, and our teacher does not seem like anything special.

This is not without its good points, as we are developing confidence in our cultivation of the Way and a sense of boldness that makes the world appear less intimidating. But because we are susceptible to taking a light view of our teacher and, with a bit of knowledge, to taking a light view of the world, we contract the dreaded "disease of middle capacity." We see many cases where people who are not aware of this phenomenon come under the impression at this point that their practice is complete and pursue unconstrained action, engaging in such self-indulgent behavior as mimicking a buddha's great freedom.

Over the course of our mind-practice, we discover that Māra lies buried within our minds. Some individuals who have not yet reached the stage of Māra defeated—where they have fought with and completely overcome Māra—nevertheless come under the misapprehension that they have subdued the three poison minds of greed, hatred, and delusion. At this point, they neglect their practice and act and stop as they please.

We must be aware that this period presents a truly fearsome test for the practitioner. Unless we invest great importance in the precepts and in cause and effect and receive rigorous instruction from a teacher to help us move past this barrier, we will end up going astray forever as a practitioner.

I believe that some seventy to eighty percent of people who begin mind-practice and cultivation of the Way do not properly move past this middle capacity. They do not become buddhas and bodhisattvas, and they end up wandering back to the road of transgression, evil, and samsara.

Among the dharma instructions of Master Taesan, we find the phrase, "If one is unconstrained within constraint, constrained in the absence of constraint, and free of non-constraint in the absence of constraint, this is the true absence of constraint." When engaging in mind-practice, the person who cultivates the Way must invest great importance in the precepts and in cause and effect and develop the feeling that there is no obstacle even when an obstacle exists. When we feel that no obstacle is present, and when we engage in individual actions, we must assess our actions against cause and effect and the precepts. Even when there is no obstacle, then, we must live as if this were not the case. In other words, we should live amid the feeling that no obstacle exists. Yet when we produce a mind and act, we must produce the proper mind in terms of the precepts and of cause and effect. Master Taesan said that this is how one becomes well trained in the lack of constraint and the presence of constraint and attains true freedom of the mind, so we should refer closely to this.

For the most part, sentient beings are led by greed to fixate on anything and everything. The practitioner, however, seeks to be free of obstacles in everything and to let go of attachment. The problem, then, is that while the sentient being cannot be free because of attachment, the practitioner suffers from the disease of regarding everything as troublesome and seeking to let go of it.

The desire to let go—what an easy disease this is for the

practitioner to catch! If we think about it, this, too, is a kind of attachment—an attachment to letting go. Thus the practitioner of the Way contracts the disease of non-constraint, evading responsibility and taking a light view of his duties.

True non-constraint practice means knowing how to let go of what needs to be let go of and how to hold on to what needs to be held on to, so that we can hold on in our actions while at the same time having the ability to let go of something when it is time to do so, no matter how pleasant it may be. Likewise, we should be able to hold on to the responsibilities and duties we must hold on to, no matter how unpleasant, yet do so with a feeling of having let go even as we hold on.

When a person does business, he is always pleased to develop a certain degree of wherewithal from working diligently and gaining credit from people. Yet it is said that this is actually the time when he must be most careful, for in many cases the credit he has obtained will lead him to expand his business, feeling no fear of debt, and he will end up failing.

Likewise, when the person engaging in mind-practice works hard to cultivate the Way and accumulate merits, he gradually becomes aware of things he did not know and gains the recognition of others. He, too, comes under the mistaken impression that he has completely subdued the three poison minds and he takes a light view of teachers and the world, as well as of cause and effect. He violates the precepts that he should be upholding, and he commits serious transgressions and evil on the pretext of unconstrained action. When someone is largely unaware, the scope of his transgressions and evil is not great, but the transgressions and evil of the leader have an influence that is enormous and profound, making his transgressions all the more grievous when they occur. We must be truly cautious of inexpert unconstrained action.

# MISAPPREHENSIONS ABOUT
# SEEING THE NATURE

As a practitioner engages in mind-practice, there are times when his mind does not function as he wishes, and he acts as a plaything of his environment or finds himself bewildered by strange and inexplicable feelings. But if he continues for a long time accumulating merits—performing seated meditation, reciting the Buddha's name, offering mental affirmation, engaging in practice to assess mindfulness and unmindfulness, and so forth—that mind, for all its jumping about like a monkey in a tree, will quiet down. Order will be restored, and his mind will function as he wishes.

In the process, he will gain some general sense of his original mind and come to understand what the discriminating mind is. If he engages in further exertion, he will develop an interest in critical phases, such as what all the buddhas of the three periods did to become buddhas.

Thus questions arise as to what the Il-Won-Sang mind is, what the nature of the true mind is, what the mind of supremely happy ultimate bliss is. If we hold on to those questions and accumulate merits over a long period of time in an effort to understand, we will finally come to know our original mind. While there are some cases in which we gain understanding all at once, if we repeat the experience several times—saying to ourselves, "Aha! This is the truth mind"—we will have such a profound understanding of the original mind that there can no longer be any question. This is called "seeing the nature." It means that we have understood or sensed the nature that is our original mind.

The original mind is ever-calm and ever-alert, its discriminations evident even in its tranquility. Though it is empty, it is alive and animated in its emptiness. Yet we find cases where someone gains an understanding of this mind and comes to believe that he has completed his practice; he disregards cause and effect and the precepts and fails to engage in repentance practice. In this situation, he will ultimately be unable to achieve great practice. If he errs, he may neglect his repentance practice and commit transgressions externally.

In a sense, seeing the nature could be described as the beginning of true practice. Even if we have understood our original mind, and how it is the same as the buddha's, it is difficult to hold on to that mind when we encounter the sensory conditions of the five desires. For even those who are aware have difficulty breaking their old habits all at once. After we have seen the nature, we must then engage in focused practice with nourishing the nature, which will allow us to preserve that mind in both action and rest and thereby eliminate the three poison minds that form the roots of transgressions and evil, if we are to finally be free from transgressions and evil.

Externally, practice with nourishing the nature means preserving our original mind just as it is, without allowing it to be tainted even slightly or to align itself with the sensory conditions outside that cause tumult, the dark conditions that lead to delusion, the sensory conditions that cause our minds to err. Internally, it means extinguishing the distracting thoughts and desires that arise so that we do not lose any of our original buddha nature. Thus, it is practice that we engage in so that all good or bad sensory conditions, all sensory conditions of hatred and love, become one single flavor. For this reason, the person who has engaged in true practice with seeing the nature must work to accumulate merits so that he maintains that mind equally between action and rest.

Even when we have attained that no-mind in all situations, it is not easy to face a chaotic temporal world and form judgments about what is just, what approach represents the middle way, what is most suited to the proper sequence, or what is beneficial both to ourselves and to other people. If, after seeing the nature, we are unable to awaken to the truth that is the retribution and response of cause and effect (the alternating predominance of *yin* and *yang*), the principle of the universe and of human right and wrong, benefit and harm, then we cannot undertake the buddha's tathāgata or middle way actions.

In the *Diamond Sutra*, we find the words, "Discrimination should be allowed through the unconditioned dharma." What this says is that even if we have understood the unconditioned dharma and preserved it well to become an enlightened one unencumbered by affairs, this is not the end of our practice—one only becomes a buddha by practicing with the dharma of discrimination and using the appropriate discrimination when delivering all sentient beings.

Śākyamuni Buddha and Confucius showed the appropriate mercy when offering that mercy and benevolence to sentient beings, and they delivered sermons that were suited to each particular person. This was possible because they had gained an understanding of the principle by which the world changes— that is, that the universe transforms according to the alternating predominance of *yin* and *yang*.

Thus we must engage in practice with nourishing the nature even after seeing it, and we must engage in the practice of the principle of cause and effect (the alternating predominance of *yin* and *yang*) so that we can generate the right mind for the principle when producing and using our minds. Furthermore, we must engage in practice with commanding the nature, with the aim of applying that principle of cause and effect in our judgments and the practice of those judgments. Thus we must not halt our practice, and still less should we neglect our repentance practice, simply because we have succeeded to some small degree in seeing the nature.

To reiterate, even if we have seen the nature, this does not mean that we have awakened to cause and effect, nor does it mean that we have achieved nourishing and commanding of the nature. We may still have lingering bad habits from a previous life, and we may have committed some wrong in a past life whose karmic power manifests itself when we have not yet instilled the capability of responding to it, obliging us to once again suffer the pain of samsara. Because of this, we must not shirk cultivation of the Way—for example, the composition of transmission verses—as though our practice is complete simply by dint of having seen the nature.

# Even if One Has Achieved Buddhahood

Because they have not achieved great enlightenment to the truth, the practitioners of the Way during the Latter Day of the Law believe that it is possible to avoid karmic retribution if one becomes a buddha. This is the immature belief of people who do not understand the truth.

There are two types of karmic retribution. One has to do with the karma that we have stored by instilling habits within ourselves. For example, we may have produced many greedy minds and instilled a habit in that way, or we may have instilled the habit of being quick to anger, or we may have repeated false minds over and over until that became a habit, or we may have produced many debauched minds in previous lives that became stored up in our minds, or we may have had a stubborn temperament and thus developed a coarse disposition. This self-karma often melts away in the light of the wisdom of self-nature when we achieve great enlightenment, so it may be possible to go about extinguishing it.

The other has to do with the fixed karma planted within the minds of others when they have suffered some harm or enjoyed some benefit through our actions, bad or good. With this fixed karma, the right to exercise it lies not with us but with the other person. We are therefore obliged to receive that karma in return in accordance with the other person's retaliation mind, even if we have become buddhas. Of course, it is said of buddhas that their ability is so great that they are able to reduce the amount received or adjust the timing of it, but that it is not extinguished completely.

Huineng was someone with the dharma power of the buddha. One of the pupils of Shenxiu—another monk who had formed an antagonistic relationship with Huineng—was a novice monk named Zhang Xingchang. One day, Xingchang snuck into Huineng's bedroom with the intent to do him harm. On that day, Huineng sensed a strange bloodlust around him. He left his bedroom as it was and hid off to the side. When Xingchang made to harm him with the knife, Huineng said, "In a previous life, I incurred a debt to you of ten lings of silver, but there exists no karmic retribution for me to suffer death at your hand, so you cannot kill me. So take the ten lings of silver that I owe you." With that, he handed the silver to Xingchang. Xingchang, experienced a strong sense of the dharma power of Huineng. He repented of his error and felt the wish to become Huineng's student, and he would later go on to study under the monk, accomplishing great practice and becoming a noted disciple.

In this way, even when we achieve buddhahood and come to possess a dharma power like that of the buddha, our fixed karma created with others is not fully extinguished. Even a buddha must be careful of fixed karma created in the past coming back to him, and when it does come, he submits to it stoically and strives to turn the foe into a benefactor.

We must therefore understand the principle whereby all of us must receive in turn the fixed karma, good and bad, that we create with others, and we must strive to avoid creating bad karma with others. Also, we must work to mitigate what we receive when we are forced to accept what we have created, and as we receive it we must strive to turn these affinities into good affinities.

In the Zen collection *The Gateless Gate*, we find the kōan of "Baizhang's Wild Fox." When the Zen master Baizhang delivered his sermons, it says, an old man would often come and listen intently to his dharma instruction. One day, he told Baizhang that he was not a human being, that he was actually a fox. Originally, he said, he had been an esteemed monk back in the distant past. At that time, a student came to him and asked, "Does the person who cultivates the Way with great devotion not fall into cause and effect?"

"He does not," the monk replied. The result was that he had

received the retribution of living for 500 lifetimes as a fox for having improperly taught the truth.

"What answer should I have given?" he asked Baizhang.

Baizhang replied, "The person who has cultivated the Way well is not unaware of cause and effect."

The old man had a great realization and said, "Now I have rid myself of this fox's body." He paid his respects and left. A few days later, the body of a fox was discovered on the mountain.

The great practitioner of the Way, someone who has achieved right enlightenment, may come to a radiant understanding of the principle of cause and effect and accommodate it or put it to use, but he cannot live his life outside the reach of karmic retribution in accordance with cause and effect.

# CHAPTER IV

# The Method of Repentance

The method of repentance is of two types: repentance by action and repentance by principle. "Repentance by action" means that you sincerely repent from past mistakes before the Three Jewels and practice day by day all types of wholesome actions. "Repentance by principle" means that, awakening to that realm in which the nature of transgressions is originally void, you internally remove all defilements and idle thoughts. People who seek to free themselves of transgressions and evil forever must practice both in tandem: externally, they must continue to practice all types of good karma while, internally, they must simultaneously remove their own greed, hatred, and delusion.

Focus on

- How to perform repentance
- What kind of repentance we have performed thus far in our lives
- How we should supplement it in order to engage in true repentance and be forever free from transgressive karma

Broadly speaking, there are two methods of repentance: repentance by action and repentance by principle.

The practice of repentance by action means looking back on a life spent creating bad karma, repenting from it, and, with a newfound sense of determination, boldly ceasing to create such karma and engaging in actions to create good karma. The practice of repentance by principle means awakening to the principle whereby we create transgressive karma, learning how to dwell in a mind free of transgression, and removing the greed, hatred, and delusion that constitute a cluster of transgressive karma.

The practice of repentance by action is akin to practice with buddha offerings and corresponds to "Choice in Action" in the Threefold Study, as it involves doing good deeds externally for another party, the specific object of the Fourfold Grace, and creating blessings in that way. The practice of repentance by principle, in contrast, involves practicing to achieve liberation from transgressive karma by awakening internally to the fundamental principles of transgression; it could therefore be described as akin to cultivation of the Way and as corresponding to "Inquiry into Human Affairs and Universal Principles" and "Cultivating the Spirit" in the Threefold Study.

Let us now examine each in greater detail.

# ON REPENTANCE BY ACTION

When, in the course of his life, he has committed some error, endured some loss, or suffered some insupportable humiliation, the ordinary human salves the feelings of having been done wrong by insulting the other person, believing that he is luckless, resenting the social structure, and blaming political leaders. And when such a thing happens again, he repeats throughout his life this experience of erring, suffering harm, and enduring insupportable humiliation.

Amid this process, there are times when some occasion—perhaps reading a book or hearing the words of a sage—prompts a kind of realization, so that he looks back upon his life and engages in profound reflection. Perhaps he suffers some major wound to his pride, and this leads him to ruminate over what caused his error and to strive not to repeat the same mistake. As he ponders matters more deeply, thinking about his life and principles, he enters the gate of religion, where he hears many dharma instructions. Faith arises within him, or he comes to understand the doctrine and live a life of practice. He begins the process of repentance and cultivation of the Way.

Of course, there are also people who take refuge in the gate of religion from their youth, living amid an atmosphere that encourages faith and practice, and who happen to discover in the process that they are living in the midst of transgressive karma. This leads them to resolve to lead a new life and to engage in repentance and cultivation of the Way. Also, there are people who naturally come to know the fear of transgressive karma due to their outstanding spiritual capacity, initiating a life of good works and thus practicing repentance and cultivating the Way.

The important thing is that we must make a firm determination to repent. It is vital that we understand how great a danger our lives are in, how we spend our lives floundering in the morass of transgression, and that we establish the firmest of determinations to change course toward a new life, going from the life of the ordinary human to that of a buddha or a bodhisattva.

Once we have erred, we cannot fully escape from transgressions and evil merely through some vague life of faith, expecting to receive succor simply through the power of others. Often, a child will commit an error and then come crying and pleading to his parents, who comfort him and resolve everything for him. Through this method of faith alone, it may be possible to obtain short-term comfort, but it is impossible to escape completely from transgressions and evil.

Repentance practice must therefore begin with the understanding that we are obliged to receive in kind the transgressive karma we have created and that the total solution to this must be undertaken by ourselves, with a great and fundamental resolution that is capable of reversing our mistake.

Repentance by action means reflecting deeply on our personality and on our surrounding environment, awakening with certainty to the fact that we cannot free ourselves from transgressions and evil if we do not reform ourselves, and resolving to live a new life. It also means cleansing away our past karma and practicing a new life—a life of truth, and the life of the field of blessings.

As they engage in actions that lead to punishment, sentient beings believe that this is the way life is; there is no realization of transgressions or blessings. For example, they may go fishing for their own amusement, because others are doing it, or as a hobby.

Repentance by action means awakening to the fact that engaging in killing as a hobby creates transgressive karma, boldly committing to abandon that practice, no matter how much we may wish to engage in it, and taking up a new hobby that involves creating blessings.

## Repentance by Action: Confession

In reality, nearly everyone save a buddha is a transgressor, spending life suffering the torment of punishment. When the New Year comes and we look back upon the year that was, we may see that we have knowingly committed many wrongs due to greed. There are also times when we falsely accuse someone else of the transgression and refuse to apologize—sometimes, we maintain that we actually did the right thing. If we examine matters closely, we will also find cases where a mistake we committed unknowingly caused harm to another.

In other cases, we produced a mind of severe hatred and resentment, though we may not have directly caused harm to another through our body or words. In that case as well, the energy of resentment can become toxic and block the path of others. As such, it is the commission of a transgression.

In still other cases, we may not commit direct harm against another, but we cause harm to befall him by exerting an indirect influence so that his actions are mistaken. Because these are cases of transgressions committed under cover, they result in the heaviest of transgressive karma, and the punishment, when it comes, seems to come for no reason.

At other times, we do not act alone but join forces with friends, colleagues, or family members to attack someone and drive him into distress, doing harm to his fortune or his honor or even taking his life. In some of these cases, we lead the charge and incite others to follow along, and in other cases it is others who lead and we who follow along. Of course, in such cases the karmic retribution varies according to degree, but we clearly have committed a transgression, and we will receive stern punishment without fail according to the severity of that transgression.

Whether we knowingly commit transgressions because of greed, unknowingly commit transgressions by mistake, commit transgressions only within our minds, commit them indirectly, or commit them jointly with other people, we are certain to receive corresponding punishment for them. For there exists in this universe the principle of alternating predominance of *yin* and *yang*, which punishes those who transgress and blesses those who create blessings. Nothing that exists in this universe can escape the net of this truth.

If we understand this truth and think about our transgressions, we are certain to feel a great deal of worry. These days, we can read the pages of the newspaper and learn about cases where someone in a very powerful social position has seen his reputation ruined over the receipt of a small bribe; where someone is suffering the agonies of profound illness as repayment for transgression; where someone, in repayment for a profound transgression, has been punished with such shame that he cannot bear to show his face; where people are punished by heartbreak after breaking the hearts of others; and where people suffer the loss of their freedom inside of prison cells.

Let us realize that the transgressions we have committed inevitably return to us in the form of punishment, and consider how we might mitigate that punishment, or else receive it when our circumstances are better.

The best method is to go first to the person to whom we have done harm, confess our error, and compensate him for the damage. Of course, it cannot be said that our transgression is fully extinguished simply through doing so. But it can be said that it is nearly extinguished.

There are circumstances in which we are unable to visit the other person and confess. For instance, he may already be dead, or it may be that we did harm to many people rather than just one or two.

At such times, we should go before the Dharmakāya Buddha, explain the reason for our transgression, truly repent from our error, and offer a prayer to the person afflicted. We must also vow to submit stoically to the cost of our transgression.

If we perform this repentance by action through confession before the truth with a genuine mind, this mind of earnest prayer will pierce through to the other person's mind, because the truth connects in both directions. And that person will find himself somehow forgiving us.

Among the Three Jewels, this is that of the Buddha: the

repentance prayer offered before the Dharmakāya Buddha. In this case, our prayer must be truly heartfelt and penetrating for it to be transmitted to the heart of the other party.

Lately, wireless telephone technology has been advancing more and more with each passing day. They say that before long we will have developed cell phones that allow us to watch images of each other rather than simply hearing sounds. Seeing this development, one truly senses that all things in this world are interconnected through electromagnetic waves, without any gaps in between.

People's willpower is connected between one mind and another in the same way. So if we pray constantly to eliminate the gap between the Dharmakāya Buddha and ourselves, and we communicate as though by wireless telephone, the Dharmakāya Buddha will assuredly answer and mitigate the transgressions that we have committed.

With wireless telephones and public broadcasting, transmission is achieved as long as the right codes are used. For instance, you can connect with a television station if you have the right access code. In the same way, it is apparent that when a human being offers a prayer of repentance before the Dharmakāya Buddha with an earnest mind, a code arises between that person and the Dharmakāya Buddha. The prayer is transmitted accurately, the response is swift, and the punishment for our transgressions is mitigated.

We must also perform repentance by action through confessing our transgressions to a religious worker. This constitutes repentance by action before the Sangha Jewel, and the Dharma Jewel—that is to say, drawing upon the wisdom of the scriptures—is another way to distance ourselves from transgressive karma.

As stated before, we need to offer prayers of confession before the truth-buddha, disclosing every reason behind our commission of transgression, and we must approach a religious worker of high dharma—a *kyomu*, a Buddhist monk, or a cleric—and confess our error. When we confess, we should do it with a religious worker who can keep the secrets of others even from other religious workers and instruct us about the cause and effect of our transgression and what we must do in the future.

We feel a sense of relief in our own mind when we confess our wrongdoing to someone else. When someone who has committed a transgression experiences too great a sense of guilt, he may succumb to emotions of resignation, and this, in turn, may become an obstacle to his other affairs, with the result that he comes to lead a passive and dejected life. But when we confess to a religious worker, we feel as though we have been emotionally forgiven, and we can once again engage actively in new good works. Also, our confession can serve as an occasion for gradually distancing ourselves from past karma and avoiding the creation of new karma.

However, it is a mistake to believe that our transgression is extinguished simply by virtue of our having confessed it to a religious worker. For only the person against whom we have transgressed has the power to punish us.

But if the religious worker to whom we have confessed is possessed of an exceptional dharma power, we can learn why our creation of transgressive karma was unavoidable, and we can receive instruction on how to live our lives so that we do not create transgressive karma in the future. Thus we come to draw upon his eminent wisdom, and if he prays for the punishment of the transgressor to be extinguished even slightly, this can serve as a tremendous source of succor for the person who has transgressed.

## Repentance by Action: Compensation

Human beings are born and educated. When they reach adulthood, they assume a vocation and come to exercise duties and responsibilities. Our profession can be an important opportunity for creating either good or evil in our eternal life. When we commit a temporary lapse, the punishment may be likewise temporary, coming upon us only to disappear almost immediately. But because the things that result from our profession involve the repetition of errors over a long period of time, the resulting pain is likewise eternal and difficult to escape.

In some cases, people are obliged to choose professions that involve killing. They take positions in areas such as fishing, butchery, or pesticide production, and they end up killing many animals and insects. The work of an attorney is impressive, but if he seeks merely to defeat others for the sake of money, transgressive karma may arise in the midst of his unawareness. It is also true that politicians work for the sake of the country. But if, instead of determining the right and wrong of affairs, they scheme to defeat adversaries or overstate matters, causing harm to others in the process, they will receive corresponding punishment in the future from the parties thus afflicted.

When we have created transgressive karma with the public in some way or another, through our profession or through our errors, it is advisable for us to perform repentance by compensating them in a way similar to that in which we created the transgressive karma.

For example, if we have shown a lack of piety toward our parents for one reason or another, our karmic retribution for this may be that we fail to meet fair parents, or that we face an environment in which the parents refuse to carry the fetus to term due to their circumstances, or that we are born as a child who is abused by his parents. As soon as we have awakened properly to our lack of piety, then, we must immediately show our piety. This means that we must think deeply about how to compensate for our failure to show piety before and perform repentance by action through compensation. Even if our parents have already passed away, we can perform repentance to compensate for our lack of piety by serving our elderly neighbors as we would our parents, or by respecting a relative around our parents' age as we would our own parent.

The method of our repentance by compensation can be chosen through consultation with a religious worker while we are engaging in repentance by action through confession, or we may do so after awakening to the method through the Dharma Jewel—that is, through poring over the scriptures.

If our profession involves capturing and killing fish to sell their meat, and we use the profits from this solely for the sake of ourselves and our family, the karmic retribution will surely come back to us and to our beloved family members. In the next lives, we may receive the retribution of a short existence, and we may suffer for many years in the throes of some incurable disease. It is sometimes the case that two people contract the same disease and receive the same environment and medicine, yet one recovers quickly and the other suffers for many years without being cured. This is an instance where the latter engaged in excessive slaughter in previous lives and is suffering the agonies of illness as retribution.

In this way, when we are obliged to store up the karma of slaughter due to a profession chosen without recourse, we should not use the profits for our family alone. Rather, we should engage in repentance by compensation by distributing our earnings among places that save lives or by providing special service throughout our life to some work that shows respect for life.

Sometimes, when I see committed intellectuals in Japan adopting a particularly humble attitude toward Koreans or coming to Korea and engaging in activities as an expression of apology, I sense that they are performing repentance by compensation. In my childhood days, I read and re-read the book *Resurrection* by Leo Tolstoy. In that book, the nobleman Nekhlyudov committed a transgression with his maid Katyusha that ruined her life. Later in his life, he repents and travels all the way to distant Siberia to live a life of penitence. This, too, could be called a kind of repentance by compensation.

If someone has committed a transgression due to a fault of his character, that aspect will linger forever as a character flaw as long as he fails to fix it. It will cause him to commit the same form of transgressions and evil again. Because of this, he must realize this and engage in a life of repentance through compensation along the same lines if that character flaw is to be remedied and his is to be a consummate character without flaws.

So while we are suffering punishment in whatever life for

transgressions committed out of ignorance or transgressions through frequent acts of murder, blessings will also come our way thanks to our repentance by compensation today. As a result, we may suffer punishment amid blessings, or we may enjoy blessings right after the punishment. The punishment will not seem so painful emotionally, and we will be able to easily overcome it.

The most representative example of repentance by compensation is that of the Swedish scientist Alfred Nobel, the inventor of dynamite. Many living creatures suffered the pain of death as a result of his invention, but as compensation for this he created the Nobel Prize system, which expresses respect for the peace of humankind. Today, its influence stretches throughout the world. This is a standout case of repentance by compensation. If his explosive was used for the development of the world and his contribution to awakening a spirit of peace in humankind through the creation of the Nobel Prize was greater than the loss of life among living creatures due to his explosive, I believe that his punishment will be less and his reward will be greater.

## Repentance by Action: Service to the Public

There is a saying among the people of this world: "Small thieves are sent to jail, while large thieves are treated like kings." In many cases, the statesmen who start wars through errors in judgment, thus providing the impetus for the slaughter of many human lives, and the generals who distinguish themselves by mercilessly killing countless soldiers through all manner of stratagems in a war stemming from a dispute over interests, are actually honored with medals.

There are people who unwittingly created great transgressive karma by committing such grave historical transgressions, by manufacturing drugs and confusing the minds of countless people, or by shirking their responsibilities and causing harm to many people in the process.

In this world, we see people for whom nothing works out, people who go from failure to failure no matter how diligently they work. Sometimes, this is because they simply have no knack for handling their affairs, but it may also be the result of great transgressive karma created in previous lives.

In society, there are certain workplaces and groups that work especially hard to promote the public good. These include educational institutions and groups working for the public interest. When we seek to disrupt their official duties or to eradicate such groups because of perverse desires, this has the ultimate effect of destroying social justice, and great transgressive karma is amassed.

Religions, which serve to exalt the morals of holy sages, are a source of morality that clears away the corruption of the world. When we obstruct and threaten religious groups out of ignorance, this has the result of corrupting all of society, and it is thus a truly great transgression. The effect of such enormous transgressive karma may come in the form of divine punishment. We may fall afoul of a major disaster—losing our fortune to a natural calamity such as a sudden typhoon, losing our life or our family. Sometimes, we are punished by having to spend a long lifetime suffering from severe illness.

What should we do when we have created such ineradicable transgressive karma? True, we should engage in repentance by action by praying sincerely before the Dharmakāya Buddha. We should perform repentance by drawing upon the dharma power of our teacher and the wisdom of the scriptures. But at the same time, we must dedicate our entire lifetime to selfless service to the public through an organization serving the public interest. The only way to have even a small part of our divine punishment mitigated is to turn to the holy gate of religion and perform volunteer service for the religious workers who are profoundly dedicated to the entire populace, or to perform repentance by action through great service to the public, accepting the most difficult of tasks whose grace extends to many members of the public. Even if we are subjected to divine punishment, we can immediately enter the affinity for birth on good paths, or we may at least shorten our many years of punishment by some small amount.

## Repentance by Action: Requital of Grace through Buddha Offerings to the Fourfold Grace

People are obliged to live with others. We encounter our mother first and enjoy much grace from her. Next, we encounter our father, and then our siblings and relatives. As we grow, we encounter countless other people, as well as innumerable animals, and we interact with them over the course of our lives. If we exchange only good things in the process, our relationships will consist of corresponding lifegiving. This refers to a relationship of grace in which each party helps the other, a relationship where grace arises on both sides rather than just one.

But even a corresponding lifegiving relationship of grace may become one that is good for one side and harmful to the other. This depends on how we react in the face of the other's interest. In other words, a relationship of corresponding lifegiving can transform into a relationship of corresponding harm. This refers to a relationship in which each side produces harm for the other—a relationship in which, through the inevitable meeting of two fatal foes, the effects of their actions are merely damaging to both sides.

However, even this relationship of corresponding harm can ultimately transform into a relationship of corresponding lifegiving if, when encountering that person here and now, we take it upon ourselves to suffer the damages, to make sacrifices, and to treat that person well, and we accumulate such actions over a long period of time.

We can also maintain this relationship of corresponding lifegiving for a long time without change, allowing it to grow even deeper. This is because we requite each other's grace with a sense of gratitude and performing buddha offerings, each serving the other as though he were a buddha.

In addition, there are cases where a relationship of corresponding harm proceeds toward greater and greater harm, where a foe becomes even more of a foe. This is because one person resents the other, continuing to nurse that mind rather than letting it go, and this results in the perpetration of actions of corresponding harm based upon that resentful mind.

As such, repentance by action means, ultimately, awakening to the Grace of Parents and engaging in endless requital of grace through buddha offerings, awakening to the Grace of Fellow Beings and requiting that grace by performing buddha offerings to them, awakening to the Grace of Heaven and Earth and practicing that Way, and awakening to the Grace of Law and acting according to that Way as well.

Our parents are the ones who produced our body, the foundation of all affairs and principles. They are the ones who raised us and taught us. For this reason, we must consider their limitless grace, constantly perform buddha offerings to them to requite it, and serve other parents who lack self-sufficiency. When we do so, we form an everlasting affinity of corresponding lifegiving with them, becoming requiters of grace who are ever serving one another.

We also encounter innumerable fellow beings whose cooperation we enlist over the course of our lives. Without them, we could not live. We must therefore discover the fundamental Grace of Fellow Beings and engage at all times in actions that are beneficial both to us and to them. If we go further and correct our relationship with animals as well into one of corresponding lifegiving, we will become someone who forever enjoys grace from his fellow beings.

Additionally, we live our lives in a profound relationship with heaven, earth, and nature. Our consciousness of life is shaped by the primeval environment of nature, as are our culture and habits. The person who lives amid a poor natural environment may be depressive and violent, and he is forced to create and live in a society that is adapted to that environment.

As such, there are unseen but profound relationships of cause and effect between human beings and nature. If we awaken profoundly to how much heaven, earth, and nature offer us humans, and if we approach nature with a grateful mind, a mind of respect toward nature's providence, and feelings of reverence, ours will be a life spent enjoying the beneficence of nature.

Finally, there also exists in our lives the law, which maintains social order. If we go about reforming our relationship with the law into one of mutual preservation and assistance, we will forever enjoy the guidance and protection of the law. But if we disregard the law and do only as we please, we will not only lack the protection of the law, but we will live a life that is bereft of freedom.

Thus we must be aware that the ultimate repentance by action consists not only of constant requital of grace through buddha offerings to our parents and fellow beings, but also the fixing of our relationships with heaven, earth, nature, and law into ones of corresponding lifegiving, continuing to put our gratitude into practice and serving heaven, earth, nature, and the intangible law as we would the buddha. We must live a life of the most expert repentance by action, remaining ever grateful to all people and all things and serving them as buddhas.

# ON REPENTANCE BY PRINCIPLE

Repentance by principle means fundamentally overcoming transgressive karma by awakening to the principles behind the commission of transgressions, and changing corresponding harm into corresponding lifegiving, bad karma into good, through understanding and changing the structure of the method of mind use behind the commission of transgressions. Whereas repentance by action involves building up future blessings and happiness through continued external buddha offerings to the specific objects of the Fourfold Grace of Heaven and Earth, Parents, Fellow Beings, and Law, repentance by principle consists of changing the very structure of the transgressive use of the mind into one of using the mind to create blessings.

If we look closely and deeply at the phenomena of the universe and nature, of society, or of our own lives, we can find hidden causes there such that no other outcome but that phenomenon was possible.

When a person is suffering from a cold, the number of possible cold viruses is so vast that the treatment, rather than focusing on eradicating the virus, instead involves resting until the virus is no longer active, allowing the fever to abate and the body to gather its strength. This is called "symptomatic treatment." However, because this method cannot achieve a complete cure, the cold is said to be an eternal problem for health care practitioners. In other words, while it is of obvious importance that we provide symptomatic treatment, the cold will only be overcome when we discover and eradicate the virus that causes it.

Among the people living their lives around us, we see those who are suffering amid transgressions and evil, their lives proceeding from torment to torment at all times. Such people must locate the cause and treat it if they are to rid themselves completely of transgressions and evil. For this reason, all religions have taught us to determine and to overcome the root of transgressions and evil.

In Christianity, it is said that the root of transgression is the original sin. Because Eve and Adam, the progenitors of humankind, succumbed to Satan's temptation and ate fruit from the Tree of the Knowledge of Good and Evil, it is taught, their descendants have inherited their ancestors' original sin as their legacy and are condemned to commit transgressions and evil. The only way to escape from that sin is by receiving the grace of God;

for this reason, we can only pray to God for salvation.

In Confucianism, it is taught that all of us originally possess a sinless fundamental nature. It is said that all transgressions and evil are generated because the physical nature of the body obscures that fundamental nature, and that by purifying the physical nature we can overcome transgressions and evil through the fundamental nature. The person who can do this, it is taught, is a sage, and because such cases are so rare, it is said that some people are born with strong physical nature and others with strong fundamental nature.

Buddhism and Won-Buddhism teach that our minds are originally without transgression, but that we come to commit transgressions and evil because of ignorance—a lack of awareness of and inability to recover this mind. They teach us that our lives will be free of transgression when we awaken to this original mind and preserve and use it well.

Western religions explain transgressions and evil in terms of original sin and emphasize salvation through the power of others, as the power to resolve that original sin lies with God. In contrast, it could be said that Eastern religions emphasize practice through one's own efforts, since theirs is a structure in which a person who overcomes ignorance and human sentiment through his own practice can live a life free of transgression.

I believe that there is sense in both of these views, and that a method for totally overcoming transgressive karma would combine both of them. No matter how effective we are at politics, no matter how much the economy prospers and the culture develops, the eternal question of humankind is whether it is possible to be free from transgressive karma. I believe that religions exist because of this ultimate question.

Ahead of these external matters of politics and economy, repentance by principle means awakening to the fundamental principle by which we create the transgressive karma that gives us pain, and finding and putting into practice a way of overcoming that transgressive karma through our own efforts.

## Repentance by Principle: Seeing the Nature

There exists a land where there is no transgression. There is a place where no pain exists. We call that place "the buddha mind," or "self-nature." We also call it Heaven. In the land of our mind, there exists a realm of ultimate bliss that transcends all sufferings and distress. There is a realm of absolute, ultimate good that transcends all discriminations of good and bad, all questions of right and wrong. When we awaken to this, it is called "seeing the nature."

The Chinese character for "nature" (性) shows the symbol for

"birth" (生) next to the symbol for "mind" (心). It therefore means "the place from which the mind emerges." Our minds contain all manner of thoughts, thoughts of right and wrong, good and bad. Where did these thoughts come from? We are going along with no thoughts at all, and suddenly we hear the chirping of a magpie and think to ourselves, "A magpie is calling—looks like good news is coming my way." (Magpies are considered a sign of good luck in Korea.) What exists to make it so that, when we experience sensory conditions, we immediately create the thought according to the conditions? What kind of state exists prior to the creation of such–and–such thought? Imagine it.

We commit transgressions because of a vast variety of thoughts. For instance, it is said that when the poor person sees the rich person, a needless mind of hatred emerges within him. The person with an unattractive face sees a beautiful person and experiences a mind of jealousy. We create transgressive karma when this mind of hatred or jealousy begins to operate and manifests itself through actions.

Thus the no-mind state that exists prior to the emergence of any thought is the state of the mind that is free of transgression. We therefore say that this is a realm of the utmost good and ultimate bliss.

The Founding Master of *Won*-Buddhism called this mind of ultimate bliss the "ever-calm and ever-alert mind." In other words, he said that it is the ultimate in tranquility. However, he also said that it is not a sleeping, cloudy mind but one that is vividly alive. He also said that this mind is one of "true voidness and marvelous existence."

We must witness this nature of the mind—that is to say, we must see the nature. The word "seeing" here could be thought of as meaning "understanding" or "bringing into awareness." The Founding Master said that this nature realm is devoid of the nature of transgressions. We must understand this realm where the roots of transgression are absent if we are to avoid committing transgressions.

The nature that is devoid of the nature of transgression necessarily contains within it all manner of principles. If we experienced someone's hatred yesterday, a mind to retaliate against him at all costs arises when we see him today. Likewise, if I did harm to someone at some time in the past, an apologetic mind will arise in me when I see him today. These phenomena occur because of the presence of the principle of cause and effect in our buddha nature realm.

If we instill good habits in our minds, the seeds of good habits will be planted as cause, and good actions (the effect) will manifest themselves more easily the next time around. Conversely, when we plant the seeds of bad habits, bad actions can easily appear as effects on the next occasion.

Why do cause and effect manifest themselves so clearly? It is because the principle of cause and effect is immanent in that realm within us that is devoid of the nature of transgressions. Each of us has a conscience, which judges us for our errors and torments us. The reason for that conscience, too, is the operation of the principle that is immanent in the realm of the self-nature.

Thus we can only see the nature completely when we have not only understood and thus awakened to the realm that is devoid of transgressions, but also understood the principle of cause and effect that underlies all manner of actions. Here, the principle of cause and effect and the nature are one and the same. When we speak of its quiescent aspect, we call it the nature, and when we speak of its kinetic aspect we call it principle. But we must have comprehended these two aspects equally if we are to say that we have understood completely.

Even if we should understand the no-mind that is free of transgressive karma and linger in a land where no transgression exists, we must understand the principle of change, as when we generate a mind and perform good works while keeping away from bad works, or else we will be unable to create great blessings, to turn bad into good, and to transcend both transgressions and blessings. Ours is only true cultivation of repentance by principle when we equally understand both the nature and cause and effect.

The Korean word for ignorance, *mumyeong*, literally means

"lacking awareness." What is it that we are said to lack awareness of? Does this mean that we do not understand the way to earn money, that we do not understand science, that we do not understand politics? It means that we are unaware of the truth. "Truth" here means the Way that guides the universe's operation. Of all objects in heaven and earth, there is none that does not fall into this category, none that is not subject to its control. This truth is explained in terms of two aspects: one is called the foundation of the truth, or the truth that neither arises nor ceases, and the other is the principle behind change, called the principle of retribution and response of cause and effect.

We must understand both of these with certainty—the utterly empty mind that neither arises nor ceases and the changing principle of cause and effect—before we can say that we have awakened to the truth. Thus if being unaware of the truth is called "lacking awareness," then awakening to the truth is called "awareness of the Way." All of the buddhas and bodhisattvas and sages of the past, present, and future awakened to this truth and avoided creating transgressive karma themselves while providing instruction to others so that they, too, would avoid committing transgressions.

## Repentance by Principle: Reforming the Mind

In our original mind, there is no mind of transgression. It is a pure and innocent state of mind. It is a mind of the utmost good, a mind of ultimate bliss, a mind of paradise. Every one of us possesses such a mind, whether good or bad, high or lowborn. That first thought that arises when we encounter some sensory conditions—good or bad, pleasant or unpleasant—and generate a mind to act, arises because it is caused by a certain something.

Within the empty gymnasium that is our mind-ground, there are typically four children at play. The first is the greedy mind, subject to the influence of the body, the second is the habit mind, which has instilled our habits up until now. The third, which is truly important, is the self-mind that is governed by the soul, and the fourth is the mind of mercy, which takes pity upon and offers love to sentient beings.

With these four children present, we greet the guests—that is, sensory conditions—who arrive in the gymnasium. The first thought that we produce depends upon which mind takes the chief role when we greet those conditions. For instance, if the greedy mind is the main one when we encounter conditions, we may find thoughts of pleasure emerging. If it is the habit mind, with its pretensions, that takes the lead, it may be thoughts of ignoring the conditions that arise. And if we greet the sensory conditions with the self-mind at the lead, we may find that thoughts of seeking to possess are produced. When the mind of mercy encounters the conditions, our thought is to benefit the world.

In this way, four basic frameworks assume their places on the mind-ground and produce thoughts as they encounter sensory conditions. We continue to accrete the thoughts thus formed— each of us builds up his own habit minds, greedy minds, and self-minds—and these become each person's mind and personality, his character and idiosyncrasies. Thus it is that we come to view certain people as being very greedy, others as being highly self-interested, still others as being gifted at something, and so forth.

Because we have encountered a variety of sensory conditions and built up a variety of thoughts over the course of countless previous lives, each of us has different idiosyncrasies and different gifts here and now. If we examine animals closely, we will find that they, too, have different characteristics to reflect the different thoughts that have accumulated in their souls.

There are minds that ordinary humans and sentient beings have accreted, those that the most outstanding personages have accumulated, and those that sages have accumulated. Typically, the minds accumulated by ordinary humans make us prone to committing transgressions, while the mind for creating blessings takes the lead with those possessed of outstanding character, and the free and unhindered mind builds up within the sage.

For the minds accumulated by ordinary humans, it is

principally the mind of greed that occupies the center. These are the mind of violence that rouses us to anger and the false mind that serves only our own interests. Called greed, anger, and delusion, these are said to form the source from which the mind generates bad karma. They are also called the "three poison minds," as well as "ignorance," as they obscure the truth and leave us unaware of it.

What sort of minds are accumulated by the bodhisattva possessed of outstanding character? They are the mind of charitable service, the mind of public interest, the mind of practice, and the mind of faith, all of which mainly serve to produce good karma.

The Buddha and the sages were individuals who accumulated the three great powers of absorption, wisdom, and the precepts—that is to say, the mind of mercy, wisdom, and liberation. In a word, this can be described as commitment to the Way and actions in accordance with the Way.

While there are clear distinctions among the mind of the ordinary human, the mind of the bodhisattva, and the mind of the sage, in realistic terms they are often largely intermingled. A bodhisattva mind is mixed in with the mind of the ordinary human, as is a little bit of the sage's mind, while the mind of the ordinary human and the sage is mixed in with the mind of the bodhisattva. In the mind of the sage, however, there is no ordinary human mind, and the sage mind occupies a higher position than the bodhisattva mind.

Unless we ordinary humans fundamentally reform our minds of greed, anger, and delusion that produce transgressive karma, we will forever create corresponding harmful karma and bad karma and be condemned to a life of constant suffering. It is as though we are harboring an object with a foul odor within our minds. Even when we exercise great care not to let it emerge to the outside, the slightest release of tension will cause that smell to emanate around us at all times. Thus the ordinary human and the bodhisattva must ultimately go about reforming their minds and every one of their actions, turning them into the mind of the buddha.

When I say this, you may well think, "Is that something a sentient being like me is capable of?" But nothing is impossible. Everything changes. An evil mind can transform into a good mind, and a good mind can transform into an evil mind. Nothing in this world is fixed. It is all in flux, changing from one moment to the next. The only thing that does not change is the principle by which all things in the world change. The *Diamond Sutra* said of this that "there is no set teaching": everything changes, with nothing fixed in any particular way. And of all these things, it is the mind that changes the most frequently. The mind has a thousand faces and ten thousand forms, changing and changing without cease.

Which mind takes the lead when we first form thoughts and act after encountering one of a variety of sensory conditions of good and bad, pleasure and hatred, is regarded as something of great importance. Repentance practice means reforming the mind that forms the root of transgressive karma by watching over our minds to keep it whole at all times and ensuring that the good mind and commitment to the Way are our principal minds when we form a thought.

Unless we engage in practice to reform habits of the mind, body, and speech, we will never be free from the fetters of transgressive karma. Believing that we can escape from corresponding harm and bad karma without engaging in mind-practice is no different from saying that one can steam sand into rice.

In order to go about reforming each of our mind habits, we must first have established a whole mind. We call this the "mind of practice," as well as the "heedful mind." The mind of practice must always be at the fore, night and day. When we establish a whole mind even in our dreams, our dreams can also become right states of mind. This whole mind is the most fundamental practice in repentance practice. Once well instilled, this whole mind will be the jewel of eternal life and the mother who helps free us from transgressions and evil.

We must inspect the interior of our minds with a whole mind, and when minds of greed, anger, and delusion arise we must change them to good minds and commitment to the Way. Just as we look at ourselves in the mirror every day in order to make a favorable impression on others, so too must we be very diligent about always inspecting our minds. When a mistaken mind emerges, we must pick it out, expunge it, reform it, and so forth.

Thoughts emerge according to the sensory conditions we encounter. When we encounter many good and wholesome conditions, good thoughts will be produced. It is therefore important that we create an environment for generating the good mind and the commitment to the Way. One important method of repentance by reforming the mind is through religious activity: taking refuge in the gateway of religion and meeting frequently with religious workers, poring over the scriptures of the sages, taking part in dharma meetings, and maintaining close affinities with practitioners.

## Repentance by Principle: Samadhi

Our original mind is a pure and absolute mind state. In this mind, there is no mind to commit transgression, for it is heaven and paradise and the world of buddhas. This is the mind that we must recover. We must set a time and place and enter the samādhi of meditative absorption without fail, taking refuge in the original mind and becoming suffused with it. This is the ultimate bliss. In the ultimate bliss, there is no transgression.

Christianity tells us of the original sin: Eve and Adam ate fruit from the Tree of the Knowledge of Good and Evil, it teaches, and thereby came to know shame and to sin. When a mind arises to choose values—this one good, that one evil—it leads us to weigh the relative merits of good and evil and to fight. Good and bad karma emerge from this.

Thoughts of comparison with others are ever present within the minds of ordinary people. We are constantly comparing: My friend is director of her department now, so what about me? I have a lot of money and that person has none. I wonder how my relative has been doing lately. This comparing mind! It is the prime culprit behind the creation of good and bad karma.

And the absolute mind that transcends this comparing mind! It is the mind of God, and it is heaven. If we have a mind that possesses the fruit of good and evil and we live our life upon its foundation, we will create good and bad karma, corresponding lifegiving and corresponding harmful karma, and we will become slaves to that karma, ensnared in its net to suffer the punishment of being without freedom.

What must we do to escape the bonds of good and bad karma? Ultimately, we must engage in practice so that our minds linger forever in the realm of ultimate good that transcends good and evil. This is called "meditative absorption practice" or "samādhi practice." Our prayers as well, when offered with the most faithful mind, produce a state in which the distinction between self and other is void, in which we forget even what it is that we are wishing for. Of course, in the beginning we pray with an earnest desire in our minds, asking that we be delivered from our transgressions. But as that mind becomes more and more faithful, the praying mind as well arrives at a state of sudden forgetting. When this happens, it is the ultimate bliss and heaven.

When we first practice seated meditation, we settle the mind on the elixir field and breathe. If we do this for a long time without letting go of the one mind, we will come to linger in the absolute no-mind realm—free of greed, anger, and delusion and devoid of transgressive nature—and enter samādhi.

Another method is through the recitation of incantations. We can enter the samādhi of repetition of the Buddha's name when we earnestly and intently recite "Na-Mu A-Mi-Ta-Bul," or Yeongju, the "spiritual incantation" or Cheongjeongju, the "purity incantation," with a mind toward extinguishing transgressive karma. Here as well, we concentrate at first on reciting the Buddha's name, but we gradually come to focus on the sound, and there are cases where, as time passes, we are performing the recitation merely with our mouths, achieving a selfless feeling, and we linger in the one, unsullied mind even after we have stopped reciting the Buddha's name.

During the Joseon Dynasty in Korea, there were two groups of government officials: six martyred ministers and six surviving ministers. One of the latter was named Kim Si-seup. After King Sejo had the first group executed, he suffered from an illness that grew ever more severe, and he finally performed a memorial service to comfort and deliver the vengeful spirits of the six martyred ministers. He invited the Venerable Kim Si-seup and had him deliver a Buddhist sermon. Kim arrived and delivered the dharma instruction. First, he consoled those who had died while serving faithfully. The gist of his sermon was that they would only escape from the karmic obstacles of ignorance and receive deliverance once they had rid themselves of the notion of their having served faithfully. This instruction was met with widespread praise as a distinguished effort by the civil and military officials who heard it.

For some reason, however, Kim Si-seup hurried to return to Donghak Temple, without even taking a meal. He entered the dharma hall and only emerged after he had intently recited the Buddha's name for several days without stopping. The other monks with him asked him why he had done this. "In my dharma instruction, I told them to eliminate the false notion of being loyal ministers," he said. "But then I was taken by the false notion that I had delivered a truly good dharma instruction and delivered those civil and military officials. I recited the Buddha's name to rid myself of that notion."

Within our minds are stored all manner of minds from previous lives. They lie concealed deep within our minds as the toxins of the three poison minds, and they cause us to produce corresponding harmful minds, minds of rancor, minds of debauchery, forcing us to cycle through evil destinies. The mind that forms the root of transgressions and evil lies hidden deep within the mind, emerging when a similar sensory condition arrives and generating a particular mood while preventing us from gathering our minds. What are we to do about such a mind? We must extract it as soon as it arises. And we must enter deep meditative absorption and samādhi so that we can increasingly purify the cluster of karma.

When an aggrieved mind is embedded deep within us, all we have to do is encounter that affinity and the mind surges forth like a gushing fountain. We must dissolve that cluster of rancor with samādhi. Without diligent samādhi efforts, that cluster of transgressive minds will never be cleared away.

Lately, detergents have been developed that can remove all but the most stubborn of stains. However, because the deepest stains resist being washed away, we have to soak them in caustic solution and boil them in order to remove the stain. In the same way, the deep-seated clusters of transgressive minds resist reform even after we have performed repentance by reforming the mind. The only way to deal with these clusters is to treat them with repentance by principle through samādhi.


## Repentance by Principle: Liberation and Freedom

Ordinarily, we have difficulty reforming bad karma, since the karma itself is bad, but we believe that we must do so. Sometimes, however, we find ourselves fixating on good karma, believing that the karma itself is good and has value.

The person who fixates on the charitable mind and enjoys giving to others will see a person without a charitable mind and feel arising within him a mind of contempt toward that person, without consideration of that person's situation. A charitable mind is not a bad thing in and of itself, but that mind becomes a false notion and creates the mind prone to transgression.

When a person creates many blessings, many blessings will return to him. Among those who live their current lives surrounded by wealth, without knowing the particulars of how it arose through diligent efforts to provide charitable service to others in previous lives, a mind prone to transgression comes to operate, and they become lazier, more selfish, and more contemptuous of others.

Good karma is still karma, and it can function to bring about the transgressive karma that torments us. We therefore require the dexterity of operation to wash away this good karma when it is time to wash it away, and to use it when it is time to do so.

To do this, we must awaken to the original mind, the mind that is devoid of the nature of transgressions, and to the principle of cause and effect, and reform our bad karma into good karma and corresponding harm into corresponding lifegiving. At the same time, we must engage in practice toward creating karma in accordance with the Way, achieving liberation and freedom without becoming bound to this corresponding lifegiving karma and good karma as well. This could be described as the ultimate practice of repentance by principle.

If we look at our hands, we will see that we can freely grasp and release things with them. When it is time to grasp something, we do so in the appropriate way, and when it is time to let go of something we are capable of casting it aside very forcefully or very gently. As we reach adulthood, we are able to use our hands freely, although young children and elderly people do not have such free use of their hands.

The mind, too, is structured to allow us to operate it freely as we do our hands. Some people, however, lack freedom and are bound to something, they are stuck in some place or closed off tightly, or else they are empty, without any defenses at all. It is ordinary humans and sentient beings that possess such unfree and incomplete minds.

One of the songs we frequently sing includes the following words:

"When I passed before that house along my way back and forth,
My feet somehow found themselves lingering,
And even when I began walking again, lest I be seen,
I came to stand there once again when I returned that way."

These lyrics do an excellent job of describing the loving mind. When we stand in front of the house of someone we love, our mind is not free. We also find ourselves loath to pass by the house of someone we dislike. This, too, is a mind that is not free.

We come to commit transgressions when this unfree mind becomes our master. Because of this mind fixated on love, we generate mistaken thoughts and judgments and commit errors, and because of our mind of hatred we ultimately find ourselves harming others. When we experience something at some moment, we must have a free mind if we are to handle it in a whole way.

If we have something that must be done, we must cleanse ourselves of any mind of reluctance to do so, no matter how unpleasant it is, and succeed at what is to be done. Likewise, if there is something that we must not do, we must be able to boldly abandon it, dissolving away any desire to do so, no matter how strong. Only then will ours be a free mind. A kind person can err in something important when he is bound to being kind, and the believer in principle can err in his affairs through missed opportunity when his principles prevent him from making discriminations about things that lie outside of those principles.

Among the Islamic sects in Middle Eastern countries that have recently become the topic of so much discussion, there are certain fundamentalists who are unable to acknowledge other religions and sects. It is said that in these sects' fixation on upholding their doctrine, they often start conflicts and break the peace. This also represents an instance of people committing transgressions from being bound up in a smaller good.

While it is good to overcome bad karma and convert it into good karma, the ultimate end of repentance by principle is to operate freely according to the situation without being bound to good or bad karma. It is similar to the ability to recycle materials and use them again instead of throwing them in the garbage. The master of repentance by principle is able to continuously create the most effective use of the good karma, the greatest of good karma that rescues untold numbers of sentient beings instead of good karma that is directed toward only one person, and to apply and command all of this good karma at the appropriate time in order to deliver the world.

# Repentance by Action and Repentance by Principle in Tandem

Repentance by action means turning to the Three Jewels—the Dharmakāya Buddha, the teachings, and the teachers—and, within their bosom, continuing with the external accumulation of good karma in all areas of the Fourfold Grace: Heaven and Earth, Parents, Fellow Beings, and Law. Repentance by principle means awakening internally to the principle of the universe and instilling the ability to discriminate the essence of good and bad karma and to continuously create good karma while avoiding the creation of transgressive karma. In practical terms, it means being able to maintain ultimate bliss that is devoid of the mind of transgression, and training our dharma power to extinguish transgressive karma.

When we are trying to engage in repentance by action by creating good karma as we encounter external objects, we cannot create truly good karma unless we draw upon the wisdom to distinguish good karma from bad as developed through repentance by principle. Moreover, all our efforts to engage in repentance by action will be for naught without the practice of repentance by principle that will allow us to restrain the fiery desire or resentment that suffuses us internally. In order to perform complete repentance by action, then, we must engage in repentance by principle. And even if we have understood the truth through repentance by principle and gained the wisdom and restraint to create good karma, repentance by principle will show none of its efficacy unless we accumulate good karma directly with the specific objects. Just as a soldier who has been thoroughly trained for war cannot be called a good combatant until he has actually fought a battle, the wisdom and restraint developed through repentance by principle must bring direct benefits to some person in reality and create blessings and happiness for him if it is to be unquestionably effective repentance by principle.

In terms of the Threefold Study, repentance by action corresponds to "Choice in Action," while repentance by principle belongs to "Inquiry into Human Affairs and Universal Principles" and "Cultivating the Spirit." Since we must engage in Choice in Action when we meet an object directly, and we can only do so appropriately when we have performed inquiry and cultivation as preparatory practice prior to encountering it, we must engage in both repentance by principle and repentance by action in tandem.

Long ago, there was a monk in India who believed in the importance of wisdom. It is said that he went through his whole life focusing only on practice with the scriptures and principles, without engaging in the accumulation of good karma and the creation of blessings externally. There was also another monk who believed in the importance of creating blessings, and so he spent many long years focusing solely on accumulating good works.

Many years went by. A monk who possessed much wisdom, but whose constant poverty meant that he had to worry about every meal, was walking along the road one day when he saw an elephant passing by decked out in all kinds of ornaments. This elephant, which ate only good food and was waited on by many attendants, was naturally the object of envy by many people.

The monk who had created only blessings in his past life without honing his wisdom became the king's elephant in this life, while the hungry monk was the one who had only honed his wisdom in the past without creating blessings. He experienced a great realization. He worked to create blessings himself and also delivered the elephant.

On our Doctrinal Chart, one side shows the Fourfold Grace and buddha offerings, which open up the gateway of blessings, and the other shows Sŏn (meditation or zen) practice along with the Threefold Study and Eight Articles, which open up the gateway of wisdom. Repentance by action consists of buddha offerings to the Fourfold Grace externally, while repentance by principle consists of Sŏn practice with the Threefold Study internally. They are like two wheels of wisdom and blessings in human existence, and we must therefore understand that cultivating both in tandem—Sŏn and buddha offerings, repentance by principle and repentance by action—is our shortcut to completely and swiftly turning transgressive karma into good karma, corresponding harm into corresponding lifegiving, the torments of transgression into ultimate bliss.

When we commit ourselves sincerely to practice with repentance by principle over a long period of time, we develop the one mind that is of one suchness in action and rest, so that we achieve samādhi at all times. No matter what happens to us, we do our work without departing from the self-nature, achieving samādhi at every moment. This is called "hundreds and thousands of samādhis." And once we have become an expert with repentance by principle, we treat all objects as buddhas, without any particular thoughts of discriminating and selecting between the better or worse, the more or less favorable. This is called "the one equal taste."

This outcome, the hundreds and thousands of samādhis and the same one taste, is only possible when we have engaged in both repentance by principle and repentance by action in tandem.

# CHAPTER V

# The Result of Repentance and Cultivation of the Way

In this wise, just as someone who tries to cool down the water boiling in a cauldron would pour a lot of cold water on top while putting out the fire burning underneath, so too, regardless of how much transgressive karma has been accumulated over hundreds and thousands of eons, it will soon be purified. Furthermore, if practitioners sincerely repent and cultivate the Way and achieve freedom of mind by awakening to the buddha in their self-nature, which is ever-calm and ever-alert, then they may choose any natural karma they please and command birth and death at will, so that there will be nothing to cling to or discard, and nothing to hate or love. The three realms of existence and the six destinies will all have the same one taste, and action and rest, adverse and favorable sensory conditions, will all be nothing other than samādhi. For such persons, myriad of transgressions and sufferings will vanish like ice melting in warm water, so that suffering is not suffering and transgressions are not transgressions. The light of the wisdom of their self-natures will shine constantly, all the earth will become the ground of enlightenment and the pure land, where not even the slightest mark of transgression can be found either internally, externally, or in between. This is what we call the repentance of the buddhas and enlightened masters, and the Mahāyāna repentance. Only at this stage can we say that all transgressive karma has been brought to an end.

Focus on

- Examining the method of repentance you are using and the results you are encountering

- Planning what you need to do for the next stage of repentance

- Learning how the buddha and all of the sages practiced repentance and what results they obtained

- Vowing to engage in repentance and cultivation of the Way until you achieve the repentance of the buddhas and enlightened masters

# THE EXTINGUISHING OF TRANSGRESSIVE KARMA

Sentient beings live their lives carrying inside of them a powerful desire to possess. Typically, this desire lies dormant on the inside, finally coming into operation when we encounter some sensory condition capable of satisfying it. When this happens, the desire to possess catches fire. It heats up. The mind of greed to possess burns and burns, and when we finally possess the thing we desire, we set the goal of our possession on a different course.

Should we somehow come to possess that as well, we will then seek to possess something else. Human existence is thus a history of possession. In addition, we commit heart and soul to preserving the things we have come to possess. We worry that someone is taking our possessions or that they are being harmed. We compare our own possessions to those of others, which excites minds of conceit and envy.

In this way, we constantly strive to possess, we preserve the things we have come to possess, we compare our possessions to those of other people, and when some obstacle to satisfying our greed emerges, we become angry. At times, we attempt to claim things without any sense of etiquette or shame. Externally, we grow angry, and when things do not work out, resentment and anger cluster deep within our heart. We suffer from worry, and when some sensory conditions come along to set off our anger, we erupt with a temper tantrum. When this happens, we disrupt the peace, causing damage to integrity and compassion.

But when we have accrued the experience of satisfying the desire to possess over a long period of time and reach the point where we can no longer satisfy our desires effectively when producing the mind of anger, we then create minds of delusion: pretending greed is absent when it is present, feigning ignorance when we know, feigning knowledge when we are ignorant. We devise petty ploys, and in this process of embellishing matters with falsehoods, we produce many defilements and idle thoughts.

In other words, our inquiry is not aimed at understanding the truth or engaging in right action. Rather, we repeatedly engage in mistaken inquiry aimed at satisfying our desire to possess. This is what we call the mind of delusion. When we have many feelings of delusion, we produce outward facial expressions that do not reflect our inner feelings. And when our inner mind is filled with greed, we speak as though this were not so. It seems like there is much fakery of this kind running rampant in this world.

Ultimately, the roots of this fakery lie in the mind of greed.

These three poison minds torment first ourselves, and then the world. Thus if we possess greed, anger, and delusion, it is as though we are living with transgressions and evil at our breast, even if we are not directly committing transgressions against others at the moment. And when our greed, anger, and delusions operate toward others, this is the direct commission of transgressions and evil, and we suffer a torturous punishment.

The Instruction on Repentance likens the life of the sentient being, who possesses a mind to transgression that burns with greed, anger, and delusion internally and suffers punishment in kind externally, to one spent living within a big, boiling cauldron. When things do not work out as we hope, it is as though we are boiling inside. When we are punished at the hands of others, our hearts are like rolling waves, without thought for what we created in the past. Thus there is never a day in the life of the sentient being when the winds are favorable and the waves cease.

As we live the life of the ordinary human, circumstances somehow lead us to turn to the gateway of Buddhism. We encounter the teachings of the Buddha, and we hear dharma instructions on the principle by which we receive as we have created, and the principle by which we create ourselves through instilling habits. We often hear instructions about the cycling of destinies in the past, present, and future—how we possess previous lives and next lives in addition to this life. In the process, a definite faith emerges, even if we do not awaken to it, and we come to act with the next lives in mind when encountering others or when going about our everyday life. Also, a fear arises as to the karmic retribution awaiting us, and our patterns of life gradually shift their center from this life to eternal life, from a mind toward ensuring only benefits for ourselves to one of consideration toward others. As a matter of course, we come to think about the transgressive karma we have created with others, and we develop thoughts toward reforming our unworthy minds and breaking our wicked habits.

Even at this level of repentance practice, we see the mind of transgression emerging internally, within our minds, and we work to extinguish it. The powerful minds of resentment, vengeance, envy, and desire to possess gradually fade away. Our once heavy and dark mind dissolves away to become light and clear. At this point, whatever transgressions we commit when encountering transgressive conditions from outside will be minor.

Among the karmic powers created in past lives and built up within our minds is a powerful force of affection toward our affinities. For example, if we longed for someone in a previous life but died without ever realizing our dream of love, and we meet that person in this life, we will fall head over heels in love with that person, sparing no thought for decorum, shame, or morality.

Even if we are already married, we pay no mind and succumb to the pull of this force of affection.

However, the person who lives with utter faith while engaging in practice with repentance by principle and repentance by action has a modicum of power that will allow him to restrain the powerful mind with its force of affection. He will think about the fact that he is already married and do battle with his sense of justice and morality, and in the process he will overcome the karmic power of that force of affection.

When we have suffered a great deal of harm at someone else's hands in a previous life and possess a cluster of aggrieved minds for being unable to requite it equally, we will constantly experience the hateful mind to scheme against that person and get in the way of the things that he does. This mind will rise up like a flame, even if what that person does is right, and we will exact vengeance for that loss in a previous life without concern for the circumstances.

However, the person who has performed repentance and cultivation of the Way through meditative absorption practice and buddha offerings of cause and effect will sense the mind of hatred and the desire for retaliation when it emerges and discern that it is not right. He will strive to dissolve that mind, and even when he cannot do so, he will restrain himself from putting it into action.

In this case, the power of karmic action is not completely

extinguished, but we could say that it has been extinguished to some degree. This degree of outcome can be characterized as the result of the initial stages of repentance and cultivation of the Way based on the mind of faith, where we have abandoned our old way of life and begun a new one.

# From Bad Fixed Karma to Good Fixed Karma

All living creatures build up karma as a result of their mental and bodily functioning. When I do a kindness for another person, karma of grace toward me builds up within that person's mind. Conversely, when I do harm to that person, karma of harm is stored up within him. This karma is something that I create and store away in the other person's mind.

The karma that is stored up in this way will be expressed toward me when its time comes. When the content and timing of this karmic retribution are thoroughly determined beforehand, it is called "fixed karma," and when the content is minor and its timing uncertain, it is called "unfixed karma."

Fixed karma may be karma of grace or karma of harm. So when fixed karma of grace returns to us, we say, "My luck is good," "I possess innate virtue," or "Boy, that was close. I can survive even a hopeless situation because there is someone there to help me." And when fixed karma of harm returns to us, we say,

"You always run into your foe when there is no way of escaping."

This karma that has been decided cannot be reversed and must be received in turn, from microbes and insects to the president of a country and even a buddha, for the authority to deliver that fixed karma to us directly lies with the other party, and this is the result of the principle of the universe ensuring that it is so.

When an ordinary person is visited by fixed karma that seems unjust, it is because he has forgotten all about what he did in previous lives, and so he blames the heavens or harbors a desire to take vengeance once again on the other person and does him harm. Thus we go from lifetime to lifetime meeting one another as enemies and going back and forth, with one side receiving harm in one lifetime and avenging the grievance in the next.

However, the person who has engaged in much practice with repentance by principle and repentance by action will realize that the sudden harm befalling him at this time represents the arrival of fixed karma from previous lives. He will submit to it stoically and avoid hating others or engaging in actions that cause harm to them. Because of this, his corresponding harmful karma will come to a halt.

The person who has engaged in ever more practice with repentance by action and repentance by principle will not only accept unjust treatment in this life, but also understand the other person and treat him even better, turning a causal affinity of corresponding harm into one of corresponding lifegiving. All sages, buddhas, and bodhisattvas are experts at reforming corresponding harm into corresponding lifegiving no matter how difficult the circumstances are. Mahatma Gandhi, a figure whom we respect greatly, made sure to forgive the young man who fired the bullet that killed him. This truly is the mind-set of the sage, seeking to repay one's foe with grace.

The ordinary person who has experienced harm at the hands of another carries the feeling of bad karma concealed within his mind, and when the time comes and he encounters that person, a mind of retaliation against him will come surging forth. But the enlightened one who has defeated Māra and the buddha who has engaged in much practice with repentance by principle and repentance by action will respond with forgiveness even when his turn to repay arrives, dissolving the retaliation mind away like snow in the spring. Accordingly, he will receive many blessings and much happiness from the person the next time around. In this way, the sage makes creative use of the principle of cause and effect.

# Achieving Freedom of Mind

After we have performed a great deal of repentance practice, we will become people of great freedom who have gained a complete understanding of the two aspects of the truth of the universe and are able to make use of it.

When we engage in much repentance practice, we awaken to the ever-calm and ever-alert original countenance concealed within our minds, the truth that is devoid of the nature of transgressions. We will therefore gain the power to live peacefully within that calm self-nature, to make use of the light of wisdom that emanates without limit from that self-nature, and to apply the mind of mercy that manifests itself from that self-nature in a manner befitting the occasion. This is referred to as the three great powers, representing the powers of the buddha: liberation, great enlightenment, and mercy.

We also awaken to the marvelous principle of cause and effect, which is both the principle of the universe and that of the self-nature. Not only can we continually progress ourselves, but we can also effectively bring about progression in others and be benevolent in our dealings with them. We also develop great powers of influence, gaining understanding of the methods and principles by which we can lead our society.

When we diligently engage in practice with repentance by action—regarding all things we encounter as buddha and performing buddha offerings to them—and repentance by principle—never letting go of the realm that is devoid of the nature of transgressions in any time or place—we will become the aforementioned people of great freedom. We will become sages and buddhas. This is the way for the ordinary human and sentient being to ultimately gain free command of transgressive karma through sincere efforts to extinguish it, and to achieve the character of the buddha who travels together with the truth.

What is freedom? It means the ability to use our minds as we wish. Freedom is the ability of our minds to linger in an ultimate good that is free of transgression and calm, where no discrimination is possible.

Pain and pleasure are relative to one another. Good and bad are also concepts that are relative to one another, as are defilements and idle thoughts on one hand and right states of mind on the other. If our wish is to transcend such relative concepts utterly and live peacefully in a realm of absolute nothingness, we are able to linger there, and if our hope is to generate a single mind and instruct others, we can do so capably and engage in good works. This is freedom! It is freedom of the mind, through which we can freely command the coming and going of the mind.

Among Master Taesan's dharma words is an instruction that says, "The deaf and dumb monk on Jaun Mountain experiences the mind arising when conditions come and the mind extinguishing when conditions go." In other words, the deaf-mute monk on the mountain encounters sensory conditions and produces the right mind for those conditions, while maintaining no mind when there are no such conditions. The ordinary human is constantly generating distracting thoughts with his mind even where there are no sensory conditions. When he actually encounters such conditions, he is unable to produce the appropriate thoughts for them due to these distracting thoughts, and once the conditions have passed he is unable to rid himself of the lingering notions. He is therefore unable to use his mind as he wishes. As a result, he cycles from transgression to transgression and from suffering to suffering.

There is a dharma instruction that tells us, "We close our eyes and unify with the self-nature buddha; we open our eyes and greet the buddha of all things." Returning to no-mind when we close our eyes and lingering in a realm that is free of transgression, while producing the right mind for the object and providing buddha offerings when we open our eyes—when we can do so, our blessings and happiness will abound.

When driving a car, the most important thing is to be able to freely stop and start. If we cannot do so, we will cause an accident. To have freedom of the mind, we must be able to operate it in a manner suited to the occasion, choosing what must be chosen and boldly abandoning what must be abandoned.

Everyone would like to do something with value. The mind-freedom of the buddha means knowing how to distinguish work with value, work with little value, and work with no value, putting work with value into action while letting go of work with no value. It also means knowing how to boldly let go even of something that has value when the time is not right. He also knows how to love capably and to guide someone appropriately, and he is able to act according to his determinations in all things. Thus he does not commit transgressions and he creates blessings at all times.

A buddha is capable of summoning blessings at will when it seems like there are too few, summoning wisdom when it seems like wisdom is in short supply, creating and using causal affinities when it appears that those are absent, and bringing those affinities to an end. He is capable of being bright in situations that demand it, and of concealing and obscuring what he knows if he is in a situation that calls for it. Thus the free individual is one who can freely command light and darkness.

The freedoms of human rights, men and women, housing, and the press that the people of this world are crying for—these are, for the most part, external freedoms. With such external freedoms, one can never be free from greed and delusions, one lacks the freedom of mind to love one's enemy, and one cannot be free from the karmic obstacles created in the three periods. True freedom is possible when we awaken to the principle of the universe and make it and use it as our own.

There are a number of factors that inhibit the freedom of our minds.

The first is delusion. This delusion summons transgressions and evil and torments us, and we must therefore be able to sweep it away completely. We must have the ability in our minds to dissolve away defilements and idle thoughts. Only this way can we be free from the transgressive karma of defilements.

The second consists of the karmic obstacles that we have created over the course of countless previous lives. If we are to be free, we must be able to distinguish the arrival of these obstacles and dissolve them away.

Third, our bodies generate unlimited desires. In so doing, they cause us to suffer and bring about all manner of transgressions. Thus we must sublimate these physical desires and train them into a direction with value if our minds are to be free.

Fourth, the things we know and the things we do well linger in our minds to become fixed ideas and the standards for our values, leading us to create transgressive karma. We can only achieve great freedom when we escape from this.

# CHOOSING ANY NATURAL KARMA WE PLEASE

In heaven, earth, and nature, there exists a principle according to which they operate—the law of heaven and earth. It is the law of retribution and response of cause and effect, or the alternating predominance of *yin* and *yang*. We call this the truth, the Dharmakāya Buddha, and the Il-Won-Sang Truth. Nothing within this universe can exist outside of this rule governing heaven and earth. Senseless things and sentient beings alike are born, live, and die over and over again within its bosom according to this rule. Yet ordinary humans and sentient beings are unaware of the rule of heaven and nature as they live under its constraints.

Freedom of mind emerges when practitioners from the three periods steadily practice repentance by principle (meditative absorption practice) and repentance by action (practice of buddha offerings). The weapon of freedom is truly a jewel in the practitioner's eternal life, and it is the life of buddhas, bodhisattvas, and sages. Without this freedom, it is as though the sage has lost all of his possessions. He therefore makes tremendous investments and commits sincere effort to preserving and developing this freedom. The reason he works so hard for freedom is because he can choose any natural karma he pleases.

It is said that the rules by which heaven and earth operate regulate the actions of human beings. This is called "natural karma." Among the different types of natural karma, the one that most prevents us from being free is the drive of *yin* and *yang* (corresponding to the feminine and the masculine). There is a rule by which *yin* gravitates toward *yang* and *yang* toward *yin*. This can be a good rule, but it can also subject us to endless confinement.

When a man sees a woman, even if theirs was no special affinity in a past life, there arises a mind of fondness, a mind of love, a mind of wishing to help. The woman, too, sees the man and likewise experiences a mind of fondness, a mind of love, a mind of wishing to help and depend upon him, and she puts these minds into action. The two of them marry and form a family, and they live as part of society. But while the natural karma by which this man and woman are drawn to one another has its good aspects, it also has bad ones; it can derange ethics and morals, it can corrupt our character, and it can plunge us into hell, causing us to create endless transgressive karma.

Thus the practitioner who has gained even a small degree

of freedom of mind commits sincere efforts in various ways to overcoming this desire between the sexes. He makes good use of the positive aspects carried by the man and woman's natural karma—for instance, it is said that Avalokiteśvara made use of the natural karma by which men like women, becoming reborn as a beautiful woman in order to engage in the work of delivering sentient beings. He can also use natural karma according to his wishes, for example by sublimating the desire between the sexes into the mind of mercy in a high-level sage.

Another form of natural karma sets the sequence of change from spring to summer, fall, and winter, confining all things in this world within that framework and using the principle by which they grow in the spring and summer and wither in the fall and winter, while also operating the lives and societies of us human beings so that they experience cycles of growth and decay according to this principle.

Just as the waves on the ocean have a rhythm of rising and falling and the mountains have curves and bends that rise and fall, natural karma exists to maintain an appropriate balance by causing descent where there is ascent and causing repletion when there is emptiness. According to this natural karma, ordinary humans live within a fate of up-and-down movement upon the waves of creation and destruction, prosperity and decay. The sage, in contrast, may follow natural karma, but he uses it to perpetuate success at all times. When decay is inevitable, he has the power to rest with a spirit of liberation, and at the same time to hasten the arrival of the next creation and prosperity.

# COMMANDING
# BIRTH AND DEATH AT WILL

For human beings, the most important thing is life. We would not trade our life for anything, no matter how precious. Yet as precious as life is, death visits us when its time comes. This process of birth, aging, sickness, and death is both natural karma and fixed karma. It is the providence of the universe that what is born ages, sickens, and dies, and what has died is born again. This is a rule and natural karma that no one can defy.

However, our life can be prolonged or shortened according to the karma we create. We can depart this world in comfort or in pain—something that is decided by fixed karma according to how we have used our mind and body. Life and death are therefore grounded in natural karma and decided by fixed karma.

But when we practice much repentance by principle through meditative absorption and repentance by action through buddha offerings, we gain freedom of mind and the ability to command birth and death at will.

The person who has killed many living creatures such as microbes, insects, and animals in previous lives, creating many corresponding harmful affinities with those creatures in the process, and the person who has used his mind in a violent way and possesses a mind lacking in caution receive retribution in the form of multiple ailments, suffering the pains of illness, or a short life, with their karmic retribution coming in the form of an early death. In contrast, we will live a long life free of disease if we use our minds with magnanimity, observing sequence appropriately, and engaging in actions that save the lives of living creatures and open the way ahead for them. In such cases, we may enjoy this fate even without engaging in any special practice.

If, through practice with repentance by principle, we have long enjoyed free access to the ultimate bliss that is devoid of the nature of transgression, and, through practice with repentance by action, we have long performed buddha offerings by serving everyone we encounter as a buddha, we will naturally come to enjoy the blessing of a long life free of disease. But even a buddha or a great enlightened one can do nothing about the natural karma of birth, aging, illness, and death. When his time comes, he, too, will gather everything up and pass away. It is also possible to create karmic retribution or reward if one engages in work that benefits the public. Thus fixed karma may come our way. This fixed karma is something that even a buddha is obliged to receive. Even buddhas and bodhisattvas are subjects to natural and fixed karma.

When they meet their death, ordinary humans suffer worries about their possessions, the sadness of parting, regrets about the things they wish they had done, and the physical pain of disease, without any awareness of their next life. They find themselves passing on without freedom according to the results of their natural and fixed karma. In contrast, buddhas, bodhisattvas, and sages prepare for the coming of death, ridding themselves of all defilements and idle thoughts such as regrets and attachments and living peacefully in an ultimate bliss devoid of the nature of transgressions, a place where there is no life and death. Thus they pass into nirvana with a comfortable and unimpeded mind, as though they were visiting their neighbors or changing their clothes. The body is merely the house and the clothes in which the soul dwells, and because we change that house and those clothes when they become worn with age, we likewise shed our bodies for new ones.

The Venerable Yangsan often said that he hoped to hold a final deliverance service for his mother before departing this world. He actually did so after she achieved nirvana, whereupon he departed quietly, as though sleeping, listening to a recording of the scriptures being read. This is what is meant by freedom in coming and going between life and death. One Chinese monk is said to have sat up straight as he departed. "People always lie down when they die," he said. "I will die sitting down." There have also been those who departed standing, and at least one is said to have reached nirvana while standing on his head. Of course, there are bound to be cases where people met their deaths in peculiar ways, but it also may be desirable for the truly free person to come and go naturally between life and death.

Sages may hasten their death or delay it somewhat according to the circumstances at the time. But this sort of thing is not the constant Way, and it means that they have the power to do so freely when it is inevitable.

One of the Founding Master's incantations pleads with us to prepare for the next life. This is Seongju, the "sacred incantation" dharma instruction.

"Eternally preserving long life over an eternity of heaven and earths, . . ." Just as heaven and earth are eternal, so our souls are also eternal. Our soul is unique, the only one of its kind in this world. That soul is a human being when it receives a human body, an Asian person when it encounters Asian parents, a black person when it encounters black parents. The unfortunate among us may receive animal bodies and become animals, and there are some souls that receive no bodies at all and roam about as ghosts. While we may cycle through destinies in this way, our soul is eternal. The important thing, then, is that we become according to our wishes, without our souls being bound to samsara—that we have a free soul that can come and go where it wants.

What do we have to do to have a free soul rather than one that cycles through the six destinies? The next line of the sacred incantation tells us: "It perpetually shines alone as everything passes into extinction over myriad ages." In order to become a soul that commands life and death freely rather than one that cycles, we must remove greed forever, at all places and times, remove perverse states of mind and distracting thoughts, and engage in practice so that our self-nature buddha alone shows through at all times. If we examine our minds, we will find them shrouded in the dark cloud of the five desires: resenting others, drunk from pleasure, or enveloped in trouble and worry. The only way to become a free soul is to clear all of that away so that the only thing that shows at all times is the self-nature buddha devoid of the nature of transgression.

"Awakening to this way of coming and going is an everlasting flower. . . ." This "coming and going" refers to how human beings engage in exchanges of both minds and objects. When ordinary humans engage in transactions, they devise those where they alone benefit and the other party loses, or they seek to run up a tab, receiving things and never paying them back. We practitioners, however, have awakened to the principle of retribution and response of cause and effect, the truth that applies in our transactions, and our transactions are always buddha offerings.

We must strive to make our relationship with another person into a rose of Sharon, forming a corresponding lifegiving relationship that never withers away, rather than engaging in "morning glory" transactions that quickly wither away, and ensure that our coming and going with life and death is rich in blessings and happiness.

"Every step and every thing is a great sacred scripture." If we allow the self-nature buddha alone to show through in our hearts, and we ensure that our transactions with others are corresponding lifegiving ones, so that the unwilting rose of Sharon blooms, we will have abundant wisdom and blessings, and every step we take will be the footstep of a great sage.

I believe this dharma instruction can be summarized as saying that if we practice repentance by principle by awakening to our self-nature buddha that is devoid of the nature of transgression and by preserving that realm at all times, and if we practice repentance by action in our transactions, making buddha offerings at all times to form eternal corresponding lifegiving relationships that do not wither away, then we will be free in life and death.

# THE ABILITY TO DELIVER SENTIENT BEINGS

There is a saying: "The healer is the one who has suffered the disease first." When we first resolve to cultivate the Way, we are suffering from the torment of transgressive karma and from greed and defilements within our minds, and we generate the mind of faith and the mind of practice to cure this illness of bad karma. Through repentance and cultivation of the Way with repentance by principle and repentance by action, we cure our disease, and the experience of that cure becomes a healing art, allowing us to become eminent physicians capable of healing others as well. In order to truly escape the morass of transgressions and evil, we must strive to realize the fear of transgressions and evil and engage in sincere practice with repentance by action and repentance by principle so that we become great sages.

All of us are transgressors. We are all transgressors cycling through evil destinies; the only difference is one of degree. In the process, something leads us to the keen realization that we are transgressors. We enter the doctrine and engage in true practice with repentance by action and repentance by principle; at this time, it is crucial that we remain ever watchful to know whether we are proceeding now on the path of transgressions and evil or on the path of freedom.

One of Master Taesan's dharma instructions left a very profound impression upon me, and I have adopted it as a standard. It consists of two phrases side by side: "The patient of the mind-disease, the doctor of the mind-disease." It seems to be asking the question: "Am I a patient whose mind is currently shrouded in the mind of transgression, or am I a doctor who can govern the mind well and cure the minds of others?" Even now, I use this instruction for assessment.

If we can just realize a true healing of the disease in our own minds, we can use that method (even if our own cure is not yet complete) to heal other people suffering from mind diseases. As we go through this process over a long period of time, we gain a sure understanding of the structure of the mind-disease and the method for its treatment, and when we apply this knowledge we will go from being small sages to ever greater ones. Ultimately, we will gain freedom of the mind. A strength will arise in our minds that empowers us to dissolve away the mind of transgression, including defilements, resentment, hatred, and attachment, in the light of the self-nature. Externally, there will arise in us a power of wisdom capable of brightening the tormented and dark minds of all sentient beings, and we will be able to create the doctrine ourselves. We will be able to teach them how to escape their torment and prescribe the right treatment, and we will gain the experience and knowledge to transform a chaotic society into a peaceful one.

Because such people lead lives of ultimate bliss, freely accessing the mind that is devoid of the nature of transgression and living peacefully with their original mind, they gain a dharma power that enables them to provide stability and peace to sentient beings that are laboring in anxiety and restlessly cycling. In other words, because they possess the virtue of the self-nature in their hearts, a warm mind of mercy is generated, allowing them to become the providers of virtuous influence, but they also gain the capability of soothing and comforting the impoverished and tormented minds of living creatures. Their mind of mercy is planted in the heart of the sentient being, allowing the sentient being to gain stability and comfort by thinking of and having faith in that person, and their fear will disappear. Such is the limitless capability that surges forth.

All buddhas and sages have the ability to take on the feelings of a parent when dealing with any object or living creature, enveloping it in virtue, encouraging it to progress, and extinguishing its transgressive karma.

Buddhas and bodhisattvas who have gained freedom of the mind live their lives within the samādhi of one suchness in action and rest whenever and wherever they are. They have the great ability to utterly transcend worldly questions of favor and disfavor, and to accept any karmic retribution from previous lives that comes their way with a mind of gratitude rather than torment, so that everything becomes grace. They also regard all living creatures as their own kith and kin and the whole world as their home, thus becoming true masters of heaven and earth, and they possess the miraculous ability to command the heavenly powers invested in them by the truth.

In gaining these sacred abilities, the sages began by dissolving away their own transgressive karma through sincere repentance and cultivation of the Way, before eventually developing the great power to help other people as well as to escape the bonds of transgressions and evil.

# Afterword

This book is a compilation of lectures given at the Tuesday retreat while the author was serving at the Seoul Regional. The topic of these talks was how one might develop lives free from transgressive karma and become true practitioners of the Way.

All of us have pleasant and fulfilling memories when we recall our lives. For me, it was a very stirring experience to establish and lecture at the Tuesday retreat over a three-year period in the spring and autumn.

With the sincere and enthusiastic participation of many *kyomu* and *Won*-Buddhists, I sensed the kind of feedback and encouragement one encounters when performing traditional Korean music, and I was able to deliver better lectures than I had anticipated.

At the time, I gave lectures on the Il-Won-Sang Vow, the *Diamond Sutra*, the *Heart Sutra*, the *Ten Ox Herding Pictures*, the *Secrets on Cultivating the Mind*, and the Instruction on Repentance. I am finishing the series now by putting the lectures on the Instruction on Repentance into print.

I am ever fearful that words and writing will take precedence over action, and I feel much trepidation before the buddhas. I view the publishing of a book as signifying an encouragement to sincere practice, and I also think of it as an admonition to become more conscious of incompleteness and an encouragement to achieve consummate completeness. And I reiterate my wish that all sentient beings, including myself, may be liberated from transgressive karma and become the truly free individuals walking in the buddha world that is free of transgressions and evil.

I bless the buddhas and enlightened masters of the three periods for guiding me and for entrusting me with and directing me in achieving the great wish of attaining buddhahood and delivering sentient beings. I offer my sincere appreciation to those who assisted in this book's publication.

With the prayers of the author

## Credits

| | |
|---|---|
| Author | Prime Dharma Master Kyongsan |
| Translator | Colin Mouat |
| | |
| Publisher | Kim Hyung-geun |
| Editor | Kim Eugene |
| Designer | Lee Bok-hyun |